# Happiness Is

Dennis E. Coates

Copyright © 2012 Dennis E. Coates

All rights reserved. No part of this book may be used or reproduced by any means, graphic, electronic, or mechanical, including photocopying, recording, taping or by any information storage retrieval system without the written permission of the publisher except in the case of brief quotations embodied in critical articles and reviews.

WestBow Press books may be ordered through booksellers or by contacting:

WestBow Press
A Division of Thomas Nelson
1663 Liberty Drive
Bloomington, IN 47403
www.westbowpress.com
1-(866) 928-1240

Because of the dynamic nature of the Internet, any web addresses or links contained in this book may have changed since publication and may no longer be valid. The views expressed in this work are solely those of the author and do not necessarily reflect the views of the publisher, and the publisher hereby disclaims any responsibility for them.

Any people depicted in stock imagery provided by Thinkstock are models, and such images are being used for illustrative purposes only.

Certain stock imagery © Thinkstock.

ISBN: 978-1-4497-6545-3 (e)
ISBN: 978-1-4497-6546-0 (sc)
ISBN: 978-1-4497-6547-7 (hc)

Library of Congress Control Number: 2012915817

Printed in the United States of America

WestBow Press rev. date: 9/13/2012

To

my daughters,

Robyn and Natalie,

who have brought us so much happiness

Note:

Stories herein are fictional and intended for illustration.

# Contents

| | | |
|---|---|---:|
| 1: | Happy Is He Who … | 1 |
| 2: | Happy Is the Heart That … | 11 |
| 3: | Happiness Found | 19 |
| 4: | Happiness Lost | 31 |
| 5: | A Story of Happiness | 41 |
| 6: | A Story of Misery | 51 |
| 7: | A Story of Separation | 61 |
| 8: | A Story of Reunion | 71 |
| 9: | Holiness and Happiness | 85 |
| 10: | Happy Is God | 95 |
| 11: | Happy the Angels and Saints | 103 |
| 12: | Be Happy | 113 |

# 1

## HAPPY IS HE WHO ...

Happiness. What is it? Why is it so central to man's being? Why is its pursuit central to man's activity on earth? Does God have anything to say about happiness? Does God have anything to do with man's happiness? Can we bring about our own happiness? Can we destroy our own happiness? Would anyone deliberately set out to be unhappy? Would unhappiness ever be our goal in life?

Happiness drives people—the search for it, that is. People don't do this because they have nothing else to do. It is because happiness is at the very core of the meaning for their lives. Happy is what we are meant to be. Why is there so much unhappiness when happiness should mark our days? Why is man so unsure of what true happiness is?

Why does man look in all the wrong places for happiness? Why does man dismiss God as irrelevant when God is the source of all happiness?

*God* is the source of all happiness. How does God "give" us happiness? How do we stay happy if we find happiness in God? What exactly is happiness?

You've heard the Beatitudes: how happy are the poor in spirit, theirs is the kingdom of God; happy the meek, they shall have the earth for their heritage; happy those who mourn, they shall be comforted; happy those who hunger and thirst for what is right, they shall be satisfied; happy the merciful, they shall have mercy shown them; happy the pure in heart, they shall see God; happy the peacemakers, they shall be called sons of God; happy those who are persecuted in the cause of right, theirs is the kingdom of heaven. Happy are you when people abuse you and persecute you and speak all kinds of calumny against you on my account. Rejoice and be glad, for your reward will be great in heaven; this is how they persecuted the prophets before you.[1]

*Happy they, happy those, happy the, happy is he or she who:* These statements of Jesus tell where to look for happiness. They give us the secret to happiness that endures, that lasts, and that survives whatever life brings us. They produce a state of heart and mind, or rather, they come from a state of heart and mind that is at peace, that is whole and not fractured, that is certain in its identity, and that knows who it is and rejoices in it.

---

1     Matthew 5:3–12
Note: Scriptural references are from *The Jerusalem Bible*, Reader's Edition, Doubleday & Company, Inc., Garden City, New York: 1968.

They also come from a heart and mind and spirit that are hopeful, that know a direction in life that is complete, where nothing else is needed. No frantic search is on for something missing; no sense of emptiness fills the soul that nothing seems able to fill; no thrashing around for theories on how to be happy is undertaken.

Here in these short eight statements is the key to our happiness, each and every one of us, each and every person on earth, each and every person who ever lived. What do they mean? How do we unlock them? How do we obtain what they promise? How do we know they are true and that we are not seeking in vain?

The key to happiness is simple: we need to know that we were made to be happy, and when we aren't happy, that fact alone is telling us that something is wrong. When we aren't happy (meaning that we have peace and joy in our hearts and a sense that life is wonderful and rich and worthwhile), then we have to stop and take stock and ask the question, "Why do I not have peace and joy in my heart; why do I not think life is wonderful and rich and worthwhile?" The very state of our lives can lead us into an inquiry that has answers that can immeasurably advance our state of happiness.

We get a clue as to what contributes to happiness when we identify those things that contribute to unhappiness. Here are some things that make us unhappy: the break up of important relationships, the loss of a good job, the loss of security, the loss of a loved one, and the loss of direction in life. When we look at the opposites of these, we can see what contributes to happiness in life: having the stability of important relationships, having employment that uses our talents, feeling that all is okay and free of threats that create insecurity, having loved ones close at hand, and having a sense that my direction in life is good and worthwhile and from which I obtain peace of heart.

Life with God adds another key understanding to the quest for happiness when one comes to know the nature of God. God is good; God is whole; God is love; God loves; God is filled with joy by nature; God is giving; God is sharing of his happiness. Happiness originates in God, and the creation of man in his image has imprinted on the soul of man not only the capacity for happiness but also the innate *need* for happiness. Man cannot stand to be unhappy; it is against his nature. Long-term unhappiness in man produces mental and emotional problems that compound the unhappiness. Man was born for happiness and wholeness and well-being. And when this doesn't happen, man strives to regain what he instinctively knows he should be.

So happiness is linked to God in a very direct way: man's true happiness mirrors the happiness that is in God by his nature. Happiness is not something that God has to act at, as though he didn't have it. God cannot be unhappy, even though God can be angry at offences against goodness and love. God's happiness is so deep that he created man to share in it, and he created man with the capacity and need for happiness imprinted in his very being.

Can man be happy if he is separated from God? Yes, he can, because happiness is part of his nature. Man can be happy separated from God, but in a limited way. The person separated from God can be happy in the sense that his material and emotional needs are met, and where he has found fulfillment in work or vocation. But his spiritual needs can never be fully met because they are linked to a relationship with God.

And what are man's spiritual needs? Man is also created for God, to be in union with God, and to be forever in the presence of God. Man needs God because God fulfills man in ways that nothing else in life can fulfill. So even if man achieves a degree of happiness when he is separated from God, he can never achieve the fullness of his humanity separated from God because this fullness comes from God alone and is the fruit of a relationship with God. God alone can give this fullness to man, and he gives it through relationship with him.

How can this be? Is it true? How can we test this claim to see if it is true, if it makes sense? The statement is that man's fullness as a human being comes from God, and comes only as a product of relationship with him. Let us look at this statement, this claim, this proclamation, through three points of view to see if it makes sense.

The first point of view is from our own experience of life. When we have been the unhappiest in life, what was it that brought it to an end? Let's take, for example, the case where a person has chosen the wrong work for her career. Let's suppose the person's nature is to be calm and deliberate and is happiest when things proceed at a pace where she can remain calm and reason things out in an orderly fashion.

But let's suppose also that, through the need for a job, the person takes on a job a friend had offered that is high pressure, demanding immediate decisions many times a day, where there is no time for calm deliberation. This situation will eventually cause a deep upset in the person because the work is inimical to her disposition. The person's own body will tell the person, through the development of a nervous condition or ulcers, that the situation can't go on without doing serious harm to her well-being.

The person, once she becomes aware of what is going on, will then take steps to get work that is in harmony with her disposition. She will have learned something about herself that says she can't do whatever she wants in life, that she has to take into account who she is as a human being in order to live a happy life. This is sometimes learned through trial and error; sometimes people have a good feel for who they are and will avoid situations like this when the choice is first posed to them.

In like manner, the person who can compare his life without God to life with God comes to know the difference in the nature of the peace of heart that comes from authentic relationship with God. This very experience is a testimony to the truth of the statement that the deepest happiness comes from God through relationship with him. It can be said to those who are deeply unhappy, "Give God a chance; this is exactly what he is all about. He wants our ultimate happiness, and given a chance, he will bring it about in our lives." Indeed, most of the time, when we are unhappy, we don't associate our unhappiness with separation from God. At the deeper levels of our lives, at the most fundamental level, beyond our specific dispositions that call us to certain ways of life, the need for God is there, and this need is connected to our happiness. As St. Augustine said, "Our hearts are restless until they rest in Thee."[2] This is the truth he spoke of.

The second example is of the person who doesn't have true human friendships in life and who doesn't know

---

[2] Confessions, St. Augustine, Penguin Books Ltd, Markham, Ontario, Canada, 1984, page 21

what this means to personal happiness. Relationships with others are connected to our happiness because it is within our natures to love. Love is part of who we are as human beings; we need to love others through relationships that are loving. Persons who grow up deprived of the love of a family are deprived of the healthy environment in which people normally grow and thrive. They are like flowers trying to grow in soil that contains no nutrients or moisture. They wither on the vine. The human soul withers and dies when deprived of being loved and of the ability to love in return. Love is the essence of what it means to be human and is fundamental to our happiness as human beings.

Again, this mirrors God. Man is made in the image of God, and love is the essence of who God is. The lack of love in a person's life can deform him or her and can and does prevent the person from becoming the full human being he or she is meant to be.

We know this from our own experiences of life. Social scientists affirm this through their studies. But once again, when it comes to people becoming who they could be in life, becoming the best and fullest people they can be, we find that this is possible only through relationship with God. This is so because God is love, and God's love for people, when discovered and experienced, changes their lives forever. The woman at the well[3] experienced this love of God through her contact with Jesus, a brief contact that changed her life forever. This is indicative of the nature of the person and the love of God. The happiness of the person is finally linked to the love of God for *him*, and this love is made known more and more to the person in relationship with God.

---

3   John 4

The last example is of the person who is denied the opportunity to grow as a human being. Growing as a human being is part of the maturing process that is natural to man. When a person is deprived of the opportunity to mature as a person, their happiness is affected. Growth as a human being through the normal maturing process is essential to a person's happiness.

An example of a person who is deprived of growing is a person who doesn't have the opportunity to learn and to make decisions for himself or herself. These two things, the learning process and the ability to make decisions, are connected in that they each play a key part in developing the person's ability to understand life and to function properly as a person with his or her own abilities, talents, and responsibilities.

Let us take for example a person who lives in a country where education is available but where a person cannot take advantage of that possibility. The likely outcome is that the person will not develop to the person he could be if educated because the opportunities for work and leading a life that flows from the rewards of work will not be there. The person's ability to make choices about one's life will similarly be limited. The result is that the person will not mature in the way that would be available to the person who wasn't so restrained, and this could affect one's whole life in terms of possibilities for family life and freedom to live and pursue things that may be of deep interest that are connected to his or her native abilities and talents.

To mature from a "God point of view" is to become the mature person he designs us to be. With God, this is less connected to our education level or place in life from a work point of view than it is to becoming a loving and giving person. All people in the world can achieve this, no matter the circumstance of their upbringing or advantages or disadvantages from a societal point of view. God is interested in the soul, in the development of people as whole human beings, as people who shine forth the attributes connected to their life with God.

Through their ability and freedom to love, their interest in other persons that derives from knowing who they are in relation to God, and their ability to be in touch with God's will for them, they become the people they were meant to be. It is to mature as a person of God in knowing God and developing in life through that relationship. God brings about maturity in a person through a free relationship with him and revealing what it means more and more to be a child of God and heir to the kingdom of God. Any person on earth can be this person, and God knows each person and who he or she could be. Life with God is to mature as a child of God.

# 2

## HAPPY IS THE HEART THAT …

One cannot speak of happiness without looking at the human repository of happiness, the center of human feeling, the "heart" of man. Far more than the thinking part of man is the feeling part of man connected to human happiness. It is the heart that feels despondency and disappointment, joy and hopefulness, sadness and anger, resentment and rebellion, peace and tranquility. As the heart is, so is the person. What comes out of the mouth always has some connection to how we interpret things through the prism of feeling. If we misinterpret another's action as being hostile to us, we react accordingly much of the time. If we feel hurt by another, we have to deal with the impact on our feelings, which usually comes in the form of anger and desire for retribution, or at the very least, a demand for apology and making things right by the offender. Feelings guide our lives, form our responses to situations and circumstances, and to a large degree determine the level of our happiness.

What produces a "happy heart," and what produces a heart that is not free, that is choked by anger and resentment or jealousy and envy? Note that all the deadly sins are connected in some way to how we feel. It could be argued these are sins of the will, or sins of thought, but far more are they sins of the state of the heart. Jesus said, "It is what comes out of a man that makes him unclean. For it is from within, from men's hearts, that evil intentions emerge: fornication, theft, murder, adultery, avarice, malice, deceit, indecency, envy, slander, pride, folly. All these evil things come from within and make a man unclean."[4]

It is the heart of man that speaks of the truth of the condition of man. God sees the heart and the evil it is capable of, and it is this part of man that God has the power to "turn around," to cleanse, to make free, and to make his own. When the human heart is in touch with God, is in communion with God, God has a chance to free the heart from its captivity, to truly make man free to be able to love more, to be able to give more of himself to others, to even be able to understand properly what man is and what he is capable of. It is the freeing of the human heart to love that is key to his happiness, and it is God who truly brings about this emancipation. God himself, whose nature is love, and who created man to love him and others, will give the man who is in communion with him this freedom, this true freedom that enables man to become the full human being he or she is meant to be. This, then, is the link that reveals where true human happiness is found: it

---

4     Mark 7:21–23.

is the human heart freed by God to love. And not just any love, but to love God above all and to love our neighbors as ourselves. It *is* a matter of the heart.

*Happy is the heart that ...* What do we look for that gives happiness to the human heart? Is it identifiable in ordinary terms that everyone understands? Let us identify some things that are absolutely essential to human happiness. The first is that a person be true to himself or herself. This involves finding out who one is. Usually we do this by discovering the things we like and don't like, the things that inspire us or deter us, the things that help us to become more of who we are and less of who we are not. This learning process is woven into the fabric of our lives.

We cannot *not* do this. It is something that is of our nature, and if we somehow do avoid doing this, or are prevented from doing this, there is an almost palpable ache of the heart that tells us something isn't right. So we must discover who we are: where we came from, what our family history is, the things that our heart attaches itself to that produce peace of mind in us, the things in us that demonstrate our natural gifts, our ability to be friends, our ability to love. In coming to discover these, we also come into contact with the part of ourselves that is offensive, that can hate, that can erupt in hostility, that can seek revenge, that can deliberately hurt another, and that can even betray those closest to us. Both parts of our nature inhabit the same body, the same heart, the same mind. The first thing in life that produces more maturity in us is in discovering more and more who we truly are.

Happy is the heart at peace, and happy is the heart that has joy. These come from certain understandings of life that are true and beneficial to the human mind and spirit. The first of these understandings is that which is exhibited by most children, and that is a trust that their parents will take care of them. They assume their parents will do this, and trust is the natural outcome of this assumption, of this understanding of life. And that is what their parents generally do, to the best of their ability. This trust leaves the children with a peace of heart that allows them to be carefree, to go about their playing without having to worry or fret about their home or whether or not their parents will be there for them when they return from school or what kind of home they are coming home to or whether or not they will be able to see their friends again tomorrow.

And this is how things should be for a child. We would measure the effects on a child when they do not have this trust, when they are subject to ongoing fear or anxiety, when they truly don't have the environment in which they can give their parents this trust for whatever reason. We would say that the child is deprived of one of the joys of childhood when they are not able to live with such trust. One of the repercussions in the long term for such a child is that they are unlikely to truly trust, and they are robbed of one of life's great gifts that can lead to a peaceful heart.

But to come back to what St. Augustine said, "Our hearts are restless until they rest in Thee," we can take the analogy of the child and directly relate it to what God intended of our life with him. He wants us to trust in him exactly as the loved child trusts his or her loving parent. This is the great model in our lives of what life with God is meant to be: it is meant to be the loved and loving child in trusting relationship with the loving Father and the loving brother in Christ, built on the loving power of God present with us in the Holy Spirit. And our hearts never get to that point of ultimate peace and joy until they are in this relationship with God. That is why, when we are unhappy at the deeper levels of our lives, this unhappiness finally has *at its root* the need for this fuller relationship with God. It is this very ability of our own nature to recognize that this is absent that tips us off that something is not right and that we should be looking for ultimate solutions in ending our "restlessness."

It is the heart, not the mind, that recognizes these things, just as it is the heart, not the mind, that is able to recognize its true peace when it arrives there. God has placed within our very nature the ability to detect his absence or presence in our lives, just as a barometer is able to detect changes in atmospheric pressure.

What are the different signs that the heart exhibits in recognizing that we haven't arrived at this state of "communion" with God? There are a few that come readily to mind.

The first is the absence of a sense that life has ultimate purpose and meaning. In the absence of God, things that give meaning to our lives are fleeting and subject to change. Examples would be work or play that attempt to satisfy the need for meaning and purpose in our lives. Or maybe family or relationships attempt to do this. But jobs can be terminated, wealth destroyed, play found ultimately to be unfulfilling, relationships brought to an end by death, relocation, or falling out.

Another is the attempt to control our lives and the people that are in it. This can give us the sense that we have meaning and purpose. But so much of life is beyond our control that attempts at control are simply frustrating and ultimately futile.

Another is that meaning and purpose can come from the multitude of ways we have today in distracting ourselves and filling our time with "things to do," even "important things to do," that give us a sense that we are going somewhere, that we have direction in life that gives it meaning and purpose. But the heart knows the truth about meaning and purpose and finds ways to let us know we haven't "got it" yet.

Has this ever happened to you, where the heart let you know something is wrong? When we do something that provokes our consciences, it is that "gut feeling" that lets us know we need to correct something. When we fall out with someone, it is that gut feeling that lets us know that something's wrong and that the longer this goes unresolved and the further away we try to push it, the matter is still alive in us at the gut and memory level. These things don't go away until we find a way to resolve the matter.

There are many times we don't pay attention to these gut feelings that are alerting us that something needs to be remedied in our lives. This is partly because we often don't understand that our bodies have this way of telling us that something is amiss. But partly it's because we ignore the signal, sometimes because we have been wronged and wait for the other party to make the first move. Sometimes we feel we aren't in a position to take corrective action. For example, our work situation may be tenuous, but we can't risk taking action that may further erode our position. Sometimes we sense that something is wrong and something needs to be done, but we simply don't know what to do, and therefore the condition of the heart continues without relief. In each of these scenarios, the heart will continue to find a way to let us know that something is wrong.

Happy is the heart that is freed of matters that make it a prisoner to hate or anger or jealousy or revenge or resentment or fear. Especially fear. Fear is the underlying root of so many of the maladies of the heart. Fear is a "feeling" thing, a thing of the heart that limits the human being in living fully, in living freely, in being able to grow as a person as he or she should, in being able to interact with people in ways he or she otherwise would. Fear, and all its many offshoots, is the one thing that cripples the human being more than any other malady of the heart. "Peace I bequeath you, my own peace I give you, a peace the world cannot give, this is my gift to you. Do not let your hearts be troubled or afraid."[5]

So then what does it mean, "Happy is the heart that ...?" At the "without God" level, it means finding whatever ways we can to resolve those things in life that trouble the heart or cause fear, anger, resentment, jealousy, rebelliousness, or defeat of the human spirit—all the things that cause us to be less than what we could be in love, in growth, in relationship with others, and in our responsibilities in life. Happy is the heart that is free of these feelings. But beyond being free of these things, the happy heart is one that knows life is on the right path, that all the things that make us most human are functioning properly.

At the "with God" level, the human heart knows when it is not in the most important relationship of all, and a kind of restlessness or unhappiness of the heart takes

---
5  John 14:27

place that signals that this need in us is unfulfilled. But just like the other signals the heart gives, this signal can be ignored or misinterpreted or set aside by ignorance of what it is telling us. We have lost, to a large degree in this day and age, the ability to detect that the absence of God in our lives is costing us something and that is the relationship in life that is the most important to our happiness, that is the final source of meaning and purpose in our lives, the very secret to the fullness of happiness as a human being. God gives us the Way, the Truth, and the Life that remedies every malady of the heart and sets the heart on a firm foundation. It is the heart that most needs God; it is the heart that recognizes God; it is the heart that is the principle beneficiary of life with God. Happy is the heart that is in union with God. No greater happiness is possible on earth.

# 3

## HAPPINESS FOUND

After a certain point in life, when one takes on more and more responsibility for one's own life, happiness sometimes seems hard to come by. Life seems at times to be so difficult that the issue of happiness being a central feature of life's purpose seems to make no sense or at best is something from someone's wish list. This can be particularly true during that time when one is "breaking away" from parents and finding one's own identity. It is during that teenage period when all this turmoil enters life, when one feels a sense of dislocation, when one is perhaps first feeling rejection from certain people, when one becomes aware of their parents' fallibilities and limitations, and when one experiences some uncertainty about himself or herself.

These kinds of things involved in the human maturation process can often lead to extended periods of unhappiness to which there seems no end and no solution. Happiness seems like something from another world, and what happiness one has experienced in life can seem like a distant memory never to be found again.

At times like this, other dislocations in life create loneliness in a person, adding to the problem. When one moves from one city to another or from one neighborhood or school to another, when a close friend moves, or when a family member dies, one can experience deep loneliness. This happens at any time in life, but when it happens at a time when other things are upsetting the pattern of life, a person can become very unhappy indeed. The place where we live and the friendships and deeper relationships we have do add to our happiness and experience of goodness in life, and when these are taken away, unhappiness can result. For some people, this unhappiness can be very deep and can become a central feature of their personality if endured for an extended period of time.

This is a story of such a period in one person's life, and it shows how happiness was lost and found again. Sharon was a member of a close family of father, mother, one brother, and three sisters. The three girls were close in age and were always together in everything they did. They really didn't know each other apart from one another. They shared all their secrets, all their hopes, and all their disappointments with one another. Whenever one was sick, the others would help care for her, and when one needed help in anything, the others were there to help. They had their occasional falling out with each other, but they were quick to make up and carry on life together as they had always done.

The parents were very loving and provided a secure and loving home in which the four children grew. The parents were people of faith, and they helped their children to understand the love of God for each of them and for all people. They showed how much they themselves loved God and trusted him with their lives by always praying together as a family and bringing the needs of the family and each of its members to God in prayer. This was usually done at family meals or at their nightly prayers with the children. The children assumed every family did this and were surprised to find that some of their friends had never experienced anything like this.

Sharon had learned from her parents how to speak to Jesus each day, how to learn to hear his voice in her life through the Scripture readings and related homilies at Mass, through the things her parents told her about how Jesus had answered their prayers, and through Catholic books that she read. She had a fervent trust in Jesus' presence in her life, and even at her young age, she had a fully developed faith. Along with this faith came a peace of heart that marked her days. It never occurred to her that this idyllic life could be altered by any circumstance. She was a serene, happy child.

That was all to change when one day her sister was involved in a serious accident. A car had sideswiped her while she was riding her bike, and she hovered between life and death at the nearby hospital. Her parents were with her constantly, and the other children were sent to stay with an aunt while her parents stayed with their daughter. Their pastor, Fr. Ted, had been to see the child and them, and given the seriousness of her injuries, had administered viaticum to the child, the last reception of the Eucharist in anticipation of death.

Sharon and her sister and brother were not aware just how serious their sister's injuries were. They didn't know how close to death she was. But the three of them prayed for their sister, even as they experienced fear for her. None of them really thought their sister would or could die with Jesus there to help her. Their thought was that she couldn't die at such an age and through such an accident. It wasn't right; she didn't deserve this. She was a beautiful young girl and deserved to live. These were the types of thoughts they had as they prayed for her and worried about her.

But she did die, and only a few hours after receiving the Eucharist. She had received it by placing a drop of the blood of Christ on her tongue. She never regained consciousness after the accident, and the doctors said that her chance of survival was very low. By the time the pastor arrived, they had been told it was only a matter of hours before she would die, barring a miracle.

It was early in the morning when Sharon's mother and father returned home. They prepared themselves for telling the other children what had happened to their sister and then went to the aunt's home. When the children were gathered together with their aunt and uncle, they told them the heartbreaking news. All wept and tried to comfort one another. There was general disbelief in the room that she was actually dead. How could she be dead? How could this have happened? Where was Jesus through all this? Why couldn't he save her?

Sharon and her sister were devastated by the news and could not be consoled, and nothing could explain the loss of the sister they so loved. They thought for sure they could not carry on living without her. Life had suddenly lost its flavor and goodness. They could not absorb what had happened to them.

After the death of her sister, Sharon became withdrawn. Her schoolwork began to suffer. She didn't want to go anywhere with her sister or their friends. She was miserable when she was with the other members of the family, and nothing seemed to be able to rally her spirit. After a number of months, her mother became very concerned for Sharon's health. She was losing weight and beginning to look very sickly. Both her mother and father tried everything they could think of to try to help Sharon, but nothing they tried helped at all. This was happening at the same time the parents and the other children were themselves trying to recover from the death of their daughter and sister. They didn't know what more they could do for Sharon and discussed what options they might have with their doctor.

The doctor told them that Sharon was not only grieving but that she had entered a deep depression. He suggested they see a psychiatrist in order to get Sharon properly assessed and to arrive at a proper treatment program. He referred Sharon to a doctor he knew well and called to set up the appointment. The psychiatrist would be able to see Sharon the next day.

That night Fr. Ted came to visit to see how everyone was doing, and they told him of Sharon's situation. He had seen this situation before in families, where sudden death had occurred, and knew well the kind of spiritual problems that could arise, the kind of questions that could be asked and most likely would be asked. He asked if he could speak with Sharon. They agreed, and Sharon agreed to see him.

As soon as he saw her, he could see the depression on her face, in her body language, and in her utter lack of enthusiasm or happiness. She was gaunt, looked tired, and seemed to struggle just to greet him.

As soon as they sat to talk, he asked her, "Sharon, what's the most important thing in life to you right now?" She was silent as she struggled with the question.

"Why would you want to know that?" she asked. "I can barely make it through the day. I guess that would be the most important thing right now. I find it hard to want to live."

"That's why I asked the question, Sharon, to find out why you want to live. Do you want to live?"

"Right now, I can't find a reason to live. Life seems so hopeless, so unhappy, so worthless. Why would anyone want to live when everything you think is true turns out to be false? Who, what, can you rely on?"

He thought for a moment and then asked her, "Whom did you rely on that let you down?"

"God let me down," she answered. "He healed all kinds of people when he lived and even raised people from the dead, but he couldn't save my sister. That seemed like such a simple thing to ask of him, but he did nothing. And look at all the suffering it has caused my family. Why should I ever believe in him again? If you can't trust God, whom can you trust? And if there is no God, what is the point of life? I feel like my whole life was built on a lie, that my parents lied to me, that the four of us have been led down the garden path. There is no one that I can believe or believe in. And I am so unhappy that I don't want to live anymore."

He said, "Sharon, your parents didn't lie to you. God does exist, and God is what they say he is. He is a God who loves us. He loves you, and he loves your sister. She is with him right now. Don't you think that's wonderful?"

"How could I believe that? How do you know that? Why should I believe you?"

"You should believe me in this way: know that I am not lying to you. Why would I tell you I believe in a God I don't believe in? Why would your parents try to deceive you? Do you think that all the people over the last two thousand years who have proclaimed that God exists have lied? No, Sharon, the only thing that has happened here is that you don't think God helped your sister. You wanted her to live, and so did all of us, but God took her to be with him instead. He can't stand in front of you and explain why he did that. But, Sharon, I am absolutely certain of this: he wants you to live; he wants you to resume your life again; he wants you to properly grieve your sister and then live your life as you were meant to. He wants you to be happy again and to come to know and love him, just as he wants that from all of us.

"The thing I most want to say to you is this: before your sister died, look back on your life and see how happy you were when you believed in God, when you believed in Jesus. This was no fluke. This is what happens to those who believe in God and who come to know him through Jesus. God will help you through this if you give him a chance. Please don't try to do this on your own. It's too hard that way, and you may lose your way in trying. Ask God to help you find your life again, so that you can live and grow and be happy, and so that you can discover for yourself how wonderful our God is. Please, when you go to bed tonight, ask Jesus to help you, ask God your loving Father to help you. Don't tell them how to help you; leave that up to them. And then let them help you and you'll see that God lives and is everything your parents and I have said he is. Will you do that for me?"

"I'll try," she answered.

That night she did try to pray. "Jesus," she began, "I hope you're real and that you can hear me. I hope you can help me. I feel so miserable, so unhappy, and so hopeless. I miss my sister and I don't know why you didn't answer my prayer, the most important prayer I ever made in my life. You know that I really don't believe in you anymore because you did nothing to help my sister. You know how angry I feel, how disappointed, how lonely, how useless I feel life is. You know how much I want to end my life so that this pain in me will end. You know that I really don't feel there is any answer to any of this. But Fr. Ted asked me to ask you to help so I could see what a wonderful God we believe in. I was almost afraid to try to pray in case you didn't answer my prayer again, and if that happened, I would be worse off than before, and then I don't know what I'd do. Please help me if you are real, and if you can."

She had a hard time getting to sleep as she rehashed all the reasons why she was so unhappy, and even as she finally fell asleep, she really didn't think Jesus existed or could help her. She had a dream in which she was walking by a stream in the midst of a forest. She could hear the birds chirping and feel the warm breeze. The sound of the water was very soothing, so she sat down to simply enjoy the peacefulness of the scene. As she sat there, a thought came to mind that caught her attention. All this beauty caused such a response in her that she could *feel* how beautiful things were. She could feel her enjoyment of the water, the trees, and the sky. She could feel the breeze on her skin, and she could feel her enjoyment of it. Even in her dream, Sharon felt the enjoyment of these things. All she had felt over the last many months was misery. She hadn't enjoyed anything—not food, not people, not anything in the outdoors. Even within her dream, Sharon could feel herself enjoying things. She was feeling something that was good.

And then this voice spoke to her in her dream, even as she sat by the stream enjoying all that was around her. The voice said, "Sharon, you see how you are enjoying all these things? This is how your life is meant to be. Life is for enjoying all the things that God has given you, and that I have given you. You have all these questions that you need answers for, and in time you will come to some answers. But that's not the most important thing now. The most important thing for you to know is that I am here with you. I live, and I am here with you, closer to you than your mom or dad or anyone else.

"You need to begin to live each day again with me just like you used to do. And you will find peace again for your soul. You will be happy again, and you will know that life is worth living. You will know that you have love to give others and love to receive from others. You will know that

God loves you and your sister, and you will come to know how good God is.

"That's when you will know that God cannot do ill for those who love him. And your sister loved him just as you did. You will come to know that she is with God and in the greatest happiness anyone can know. You will see that, in time, this knowledge will give great joy to you. You will come to know that one day you will see her again. You will also come to know that God needs you here on earth to be his child and to be his person for others. You have so much love in you that needs to be given away. You need to know what a blessing you are to all who know and love you. One day that will extend to having your own children, and then you will see in a totally different way just how wonderful life is and what a gift from God life is.

"So enjoy this stream, this setting, the sounds, the warmth, the feeling of being alive. You don't have to do anything extraordinary; just begin your life anew when you wake up. But there will be a difference. I'm taking away this unhappiness from you so you can start your life again. And remember: I am with you every moment. I really live, and I am who I say I am. And God, your Father, is with you, and we live in you. You have your life to live, and to live in happiness with me."

Sharon heard all these words clearly in her dream, and through it all, there was such a sense of peace. When Jesus ceased speaking, she continued to see and feel the setting she was in and continued to feel such enjoyment of it.

When she awoke, she stopped to see how she felt. There was no depression, no anger, no confusion, and no unanswered questions that couldn't wait. She felt just like herself again. She began to weep at what had happened, and she realized that Jesus had been with her in this dream and was with her now so closely. She knew that this sorrowful period of her life was over and that Jesus did what he said he would: he had given her peace again; he had given her life back to her; he had given her happiness back. And virtually in an instant. She reasoned that if he could do that for her so wonderfully, he must have answered her prayer for her sister in some way she didn't understand.

Sharon began her life again in peace of heart and happiness. And she knew for herself that God was truly with her each moment no matter the circumstance in life. She never again allowed circumstance, however troubling, to interfere with her life with God. This was the first time Sharon understood in the very depths of her being what "Savior" meant when applied to Jesus. And Friend. And God. And Love.

# 4

## HAPPINESS LOST

What we know and understand to be happiness can be lost. The normal, secular understanding of happiness, which excludes God as a basis for happiness, is based on the circumstances of life, and circumstances can and do change. One day, one can have the best job in the world that provides all the financial security one could ask for, but the next day one can be without that job and even have one's career threatened with permanent loss of employment in that career. One could be part of a political process that seems unassailable, and then find that things have changed and one's political philosophy is out of vogue, leaving one looking for new political direction in life. One could have religious beliefs that seem to make sense in terms of one's own experience of life, and then something happens, as happened to

Sharon, that seems to turn everything upside down, and leaves one looking for new understanding of life.

Look at what can happen when one places belief in the circumstances of life. Neal was in his forties and had for many years achieved great success as the chief engineer in a large corporation. He had shown brilliance in innovative ways to improve the methods of production in his company and had been rewarded with successively more responsibility until he was finally placed in charge of the activity in the company. He was acknowledged as a leader in his field of expertise. He was personable and made friendships easily and was able to have effective business dealings with associates inside and outside the company. There was even talk that Neal had the makings of a future president of the company.

Neal had never known any significant failure in his life, and had come to assume that this pattern of his life was going to remain for the rest of his career. He made all his plans and way of life based on this assumption. He was a self-made man, and even if something happened at this company, his credentials were impeccable, and he would be able to continue his career elsewhere. And frankly, that was a pretty good assumption that no one would have disagreed with.

Neal was married with two young children. His wife was a professional person and a full-time employee in another corporation. Between the two of them, they were able to afford a large home in an exclusive area of the city. They were able to send their children to private schools, and they had plans to send the children to top universities when the time came. The couple was connected politically and had influence within one of the major parties in the country. They were socially well connected and considered one of the elite families in the community.

Neither had any religious belief or affiliation. They came from families who were basically atheist in belief, and none of their closest friends had religious beliefs either. Religion was not something that had any influence whatsoever on their lives, neither its conduct nor its ethics, nor its raison d'être in the first place. And they had no reason to have to consider the possibility of God's existence. Life was good, and their understanding of it fit well with their circumstances. Naturally, then, the children had no religious background whatsoever.

And so it was that neither Neal nor his wife was at all prepared for the series of events that turned their lives upside down. Neal had a stroke one day that nearly cost him his life. He had paralysis in his arm and leg, and his speech became impaired. He was hospitalized for an extensive period of time, and when it became clear that he would be unlikely to resume his position as chief engineer, he was replaced and put on paid leave. Slowly, he came to know that his life had been irrevocably changed and that he would be living an impaired life from here on out. And just when this happened, he had a second stroke that placed him in intensive care for an extended period and then into rehabilitation for a further period.

It was during this time that his wife developed an affair with a senior executive in her company and was now actively considering divorcing Neal. This news further devastated Neal, who had no idea his wife would even consider seeing another man. In due course, she served him with divorce papers, moved from the home, taking the children with her, and left Neal alone, an invalid without a job and without hope of ever recovering his former health and position in the community. Even his close friends eventually stopped coming to see him.

Neal turned angry—and then bitter. He came to hate his wife, who had turned on him when he was down. He was bitter about the loss of his prestige in the community and the loss of the position he so cherished.

But this was just the beginning of the change in Neal's life that would bring him to the point of total despair, from which he was incapable of emerging. When Neal had the first stroke, the impact on him, psychologically, was a depression that kept him prisoner for about two years. The ingredients of this depression were, of course, the loss of his mobility, the inability to carry on his work, the long hours of being by himself in the hospital and then in rehabilitation, and the gap in communication that became apparent during his wife's visits.

They discovered how little they had to say to each other during those times. When he was busy with work and politics and social events, they had no reason to have to spend time talking with each other. Their conversation during that time was more in the nature of news reports about what was going on in their respective lives. As time passed, he became aware that they really had little to say to each other, little that really engaged their mutual interests. Their goals in life had been principally about work and career and how they could advance socially. Even their friendships were geared to those same interests, and as long as each of them was progressing along the path that advanced those interests, they were happy together. His stroke revealed the truth of their relationship.

During this period, before the second stroke occurred, he discovered that some of those who were just below him in position at work were beginning to vie for his job should he become unable to return to work. Those he thought were his friends were now actively pressing their interest in advancing to his job. He discovered that one of them, whom he thought was a particularly good friend, was now beginning to speak out against the work he had been doing recently, saying the work was misguided and that another, better approach should be taken and that he was the one capable of leading that effort. He had succeeded in sowing the thought in the president's mind that change would be a good thing and that when Neal returned it would be best that another position be found for him.

By the time Neal had the second stroke, the plans were already in place to replace him, and the second stroke simply solved their dilemma in providing a position that would be acceptable to Neal. Neal had discovered these maneuvers from other colleagues during visits with him, and this had the effect of depressing him even further. He felt that those he trusted the most were abandoning him. When he discovered, after the second stroke, that his wife was seeing someone else, he felt betrayed and abandoned again.

In the meantime, Neal discovered something about himself that depressed him even further. He discovered that he himself did not have the power to combat the depression he was entering. He felt like a weakling, an image he would have looked down on in someone else, and he berated himself for it. This was not how he had ever seen himself. He had always seen himself as strong, capable, and independent—a "man's man." One of the reasons he never seriously looked into religion was because he thought those who held such beliefs were weak and needed a prop to help them through life. He never felt the need for such a thing.

With his wife and children gone, Neal arranged for the sale of the home to satisfy the split of assets between him and his wife. He was in a rehab center, so the need for a place to live was not urgent. Still, he had to plan on where he could live long term. He saw himself dependent on care for the rest of his life and having to live in a place where this care could be given, and so having his own home again seemed out of the question. Nor could he imagine living in a home alone, having to hire all the care he would need. He simply couldn't afford it. All of these considerations made him feel trapped in a body that was useless to him in carrying on life the way he wanted to.

Ten years later, Neal looked like a shriveled old man. He could be mistaken for a man in his eighties, nearing death. He sat in a chair day after day without moving. He barely spoke to anyone. No one came to see him, not even his children who had, by this time, moved to a distant city with their mother and stepfather. In spirit, Neal had given up on life; he had nothing that would motivate him to seek something that would provide even a little happiness in his life. He didn't have access to a means of suicide, but that's how he felt. He felt deeply that his life was worthless, an unending source of pain and depression. He had even come to curse his own life and was filled with bitterness at what had become of him. Neal spent his days waiting to die, wishing to die, and he would willingly have paid someone to kill him if he had the chance. Neal lived in

*Happiness Is*

an unending state of hopelessness that robbed him of any desire to live.

One day, a priest was visiting the home in which Neal lived. He saw Neal sitting over in a corner, and he asked a nurse about him, how long he had been there and if she thought he'd mind having a visitor.

He then went and spoke to Neal. "Hi, I'm Father George from the parish just down the street. Is there anything I can do for you? Maybe you'd just like to have someone to talk with? Or maybe there is something I can get you?"

"Go away," answered Neal. "There is nothing you or anyone can do for me. Don't waste your time with me."

"Why? Surely there is something you want or need?"

"If you could give me back my life, that would be something you could do for me. But since that is impossible, there is nothing else I want or need. And since I don't believe in God or any of that stuff, I can't think how you in particular could help me."

"What if I said I could give you back your life, would that be something you would want to talk about?"

"What are you saying? How could you give me back my life?"

"Well, I couldn't give you back the life you had before your strokes, but I could offer you a life worth living. Wouldn't that be worth a conversation and some thought?"

"Are you trying to con me into this God stuff? Is that what you're talking about?"

"Yes, that's what I'm talking about, but it isn't a con job. Why would you think I'm trying to con you on such an important subject as the existence and nature of God and your relationship with God?"

"Because it has to be a con job; there is no God. It's all just a con job for weak people."

Neal just looked miserable and pathetic.

But Fr. George continued. "Wow. If you only knew how God has been in people's lives that I have seen with my own eyes, and I have seen a lot of people in my day, you would have to conclude that there is something to the claim that God exists. But if God exists, wouldn't you want to know what that has to do with you? It could mean everything to you and how you view your life."

Neal was unimpressed. "I don't think that's anything but psychological gobbledygook. Nothing in my whole life has ever indicated the existence of a God, no matter how you describe him. In fact, it's just the opposite. God does not make sense to me. I mean, just look around you, Father. Open your eyes. Look at the world and see what's going on in it. How could any God allow what happens in the world to happen? Look at me! Just look at me! I'm the proof of the pudding. Look at the disaster of my life. Any God who could produce a result like this in a life would be an evil monster. How could anyone in his right mind believe in something like that? No, Father, you're wasting your time with me. What you have to offer makes no sense to me and never will. I'll tell you what I believe in. When I die, there will be nothing! Life will just end, and that will be that. And finally I'll be relieved of this intolerable suffering I have every minute of the day. Who could possibly find meaning in this? Get out and leave me alone!"

Father George left with such a sense of sadness and heaviness of spirit. It was incomprehensible to him that anyone could turn away from the loving God he knew who offered all mankind the real hope that it longs for without knowing it. He began to pray for Neal as he had told him he would. He reassured Neal that God loved him and encouraged him to leave open the possibility of coming to know God in ways that could change his life, indeed, offer him a new life. He said he would drop by again to see if he wished to talk.

But that very night Neal discovered a bottle of iodine left unattended, and he took it back to his room. He had decided long before this that if the opportunity ever presented itself, he would commit suicide to bring this unhappy life to an end. Nothing else made sense to him. He saw no future worth living for; he saw no purpose to life worth suffering for, and he had no relationships with anyone that made life worthwhile. All he could think of was ending his own suffering. When he returned to his room, he wasted no time. He opened the nearly full bottle and drank it immediately. He quickly went into shock and within a short time was dead.

Nobody came to mourn his passing except Father George and one of his nurses. Father George offered a few prayers for Neal's soul in the hope that somehow God might receive him. When he did so, Father George noted that Neal's death was so tragic because real happiness in life was but a decision away, no matter the circumstances of his health or anything else. Happiness had been doubly lost by Neal: first, through the circumstances that changed his life so dramatically, and second, through the refusal to even consider the existence of a God who could help him. Father George and the nurse each felt the sadness of this double loss of happiness in Neal's life.

# 5

# A STORY OF HAPPINESS

Luke was a forty-something man who lived in a large city. He was married with three children and was born and raised Catholic by parents who were deeply devout and who raised their children with explanations of their faith throughout their growing-up years. Luke himself, from very early on, remembered their explanations, their times of prayer together, never missing Sunday Mass, and their trips to shrines from time to time. Luke himself always had a feeling of God's closeness to him, always heard his father speak of God his Father, and learned at his mother's knee her own love for God. Jesus was their Savior in every way, she would tell them repeatedly, and would show them how he was their Savior from stories of his intervention in their lives.

"Just remember this one thing," she would tell them. "Jesus lives inside you, God your Father lives inside you, and the Holy Spirit lives inside you. God lives inside you in three persons. Remember this when you are living each day, that each moment of every day God is with you, closer to you than I am, closer to you than your father is, closer to you than anyone. And here is the most important thing: God in each of these persons loves you and made you so you could live with him each day and come to love God as God loves you."

Because of this upbringing, Luke never had a reason to doubt what his parents had taught him, never had a reason to think that God was other than what they told him. He had discovered over the years that God was exactly as they had told him, that God loved him exactly as they had told him, that God was with him every moment exactly as they had told him, and that he had come to love God exactly as they themselves had come to love God. By upbringing and his own experience of God in his life, Luke had from a very early age as solid a faith as anyone could have.

So, Luke never in his life experienced anxiety about what life would hold for him. He knew that God would lead him throughout his life in all aspects. He knew that God knew him personally and loved him and was calling him to be the person God wanted him to be and that God would show him the way throughout his life. He never had to concern himself about any of this. He knew also that his parents and grandparents were totally in God's hands, and that whatever life brought them, they would live it with God each day, each moment. They, too, had that peace of heart that God alone provides for those who love him.

Luke did well at school, and soon it became evident that Luke had a gift for mathematics that would become the primary leading star in his life. His teachers encouraged him to consider mathematics as his career choice, and to think in terms of becoming a university professor. His parents supported him fully should he choose to go in this direction, but they also told him that the most important thing was that he confirm any choice he made in prayer.

"Let God lead you," they told him. "He has given you lots of gifts, all to be developed and used for others, and God will provide the path he wants you to follow. You don't have to make any hasty decisions, but at some point you will have to make a decision, and when you do, you will know deep in your heart where God is leading you."

Luke already knew this, but he loved to hear his parents express their love for God and him through these solid words of advice.

When he entered university, he quickly became identified as a student with promise in mathematics, and during that first year, it became obvious to him that two choices were making themselves clear. When he prayed about these two options, he became convinced that one of them would indeed be his future but that he would have to wait for that to become clear. In the meantime, he structured his studies to leave each path open. It was in his second year that his choice was finally made, and he devoted himself to excellence in that direction.

It was also during his second year that he met the person he would later marry. He had been at Mass one morning when he saw her there, and as soon as he saw her, he wanted to get to know her. And so it was that they began to see each other, and in a short time, each of them knew they would spend their lives together. She too had come from a devout family, and she too wanted a spouse who would share his faith and life and love with the other. Each of them already knew God's love for them, and each of them knew how good the love of God was for families. Each of them wanted what their parents had, a life together with and in God. For each of them, this was the fullness of life.

Luke went on to graduate school and earned a doctorate in his chosen field. He would become a professor at one of the universities known for that field. She would graduate with a master's degree and would go into the medical field. By the time Luke finished his studies, everyone knew they would marry, and all looked forward to that time. Luke's mother loved her future daughter-in-law, and her mother loved Luke. And so it was that they were married a few months after Luke received his doctorate. He was twenty-six, and she was twenty-five.

Luke loved her deeply and was always aware of her and what he could do for her. And she loved Luke just as much. The two of them were as happy as anyone could be. They were full of youthful vigor, hope, and love. They had good friends from their school days, and life was full. Their faith was as strong as ever, and they gave God all their thanks for what he had brought them. They were humble people who knew who they were as God's children, and they saw everyone as a beloved child of God and loved them as such. Neither of them had ever missed Sunday Mass except for sickness, and each of them understood the Mass perfectly and participated fully in it. They went to Mass several times during the week as well. They couldn't imagine life without

God at the very heart of it, without God first in their lives, or without God directing their lives in every aspect.

They understood the church's teaching on the family, how it was fully rooted in God's love and participated in God's love. They understood how they were co-creators with God of persons created in his image, and they understood the total sanctity of their calling as parents. They had seen this lived out in each of their families and understood the love of God that permeates families who are his from an early age. They longed for children, they anticipated children, and they married with children in mind. Their covenant with God was totally open to his love. They knew any children they would have were for eternity. Their children, like them, would share in the fullness of God's life and love forever.

Hardships and setbacks were taken as they came, with knowledge that they were just part of life, indeed, that they had their own purpose in terms of understanding the nature of life. They knew that sickness and death were part of life, but that each was also an occasion for grace and coming closer to God. They knew that setbacks at work were occasions for learning better how to work with others or how to face situations that were unexpected. In good times and bad, in season and out, they were God's children, and they knew his presence with them throughout each day and acted accordingly.

To show where Luke's heart and mind were, there was a particular incident that revealed vividly how he lived each day as a norm. When his eldest child was nine and his youngest four, his wife was diagnosed with ovarian cancer. The effect on the whole family was traumatic. Her parents came to be with her as she was hospitalized and to help take care of the children. Luke's parents did as well, so that Luke had the time to be with her, especially during the times of further assessments of the illness and during times of treatment and her reaction to it. She was extremely ill and in danger of dying.

Luke found himself worried about his wife and his children. What would he do if she died? How would he manage the children without her? He felt such emptiness come over him at even the thought of the possibility of life without her. They were so close in everything: in their beliefs, in their thinking, in how they felt about the most important things in life, in their love of life, and in their commitment to God and to each other. He just couldn't visualize life without her love, her companionship, her being there for him and the children. If there was ever a time when he needed God's help in facing difficulty, this was the time. He wept often, and he cherished the encouragement he and his wife received from their parents, closest friends, and pastor.

He would bring all of this into his prayer time each night. All that he felt, all that he worried about, all the practical matters that had to be decided on each day, he brought to his time with his Father and with Jesus, his Savior.

"Lord, I know that you have her in your mind and heart, and that you want the very best for her. I know you have the two of us in your heart and mind, and our children. I know that you have your perfect will for her, and I join in your will for her. I hope that includes her recovery to full health. I pray for this because of my need for her and the need of the children for her."

Here he stopped because he was too emotional to continue. He could feel the depth of his love for his wife and of his need for her. He knew how much she loved him and each of the children. He had no words to express this and simply wept as he felt these things. Through all of it, he could sense the presence of God comforting him. He knew how much God loved each of them and how much he was there for them. At the end of his prayer time, he again placed everything in God's loving hands, knowing that God would bring about the best possible outcome for them.

Each night it was the same. His prayer time would be especially intense when he had spent time at the hospital with his wife, when the two of them would speak in the most personal terms of their love for each other and of the children. She was very concerned for the children during her illness, and she knew that she was in danger. She would tell him what was important for the children during this time and who she thought could best take care of them. She wanted to see them as often as possible, and the five of them spent as much time together as possible in the circumstance.

Their pastor would bring communion to her each day, or have someone come when he couldn't. She had the Sacrament of the Sick and felt that she was totally in God's hands. They discussed with her doctors the best possible scenarios for treatment and recovery and made decisions together on what they thought would be the best way forward. During the worst of the time, when she had an operation to remove malignant tissue, Luke took time off from work to be with her through her recovery.

Throughout this period, Luke never lost hope or love or faith. He never once thought that God wasn't with them and totally involved with all aspects of life during that period. He spent time with the children, and they prayed together for her. The children saw and felt his peace of heart, his quiet assurance in God's love and presence. They too prayed as he did, asking God to help their mother become well again and to help them love her all the more during this period and to help them help each other while their mother was away from them. Love among them was never stronger than during this period when each of them came to the help of the others and when they were especially sensitive to what the others were feeling. Luke was so proud of his children at this time, and they could feel his pride in them.

It turned out that the operation was a complete success. They apparently had assessed the extent of the cancer properly and had removed it through the operation. She had some further treatment, and after two years, they told her that they were confident she was freed of cancer. They told her to get regular checkups, and if she remained cancer free after so many years, she had a high probability of being cancer-free for life.

Throughout this time, the family rejoiced at her recovery and gave God thanks for bringing her through safely. The whole period intensified the love within the family and the faith level of the whole family. Never was there a time when desolation or depression or despair entered into the life of any of them. Never were they without hope or love or faith. Never did they have a sense that God had abandoned them or was not in control of the ship. Each of them had the peace that Christ gives to those in communion with him,

*Happiness Is*

and they gave this sense to all who came in contact with them, whether in the hospital, the parish, the workplace, or school. All who knew them saw this quality about them and were inspired by it.

When Luke was old and he and his wife were retired and enjoying their grandchildren, they looked at what had been produced in the lives of their children through their life in, with, and through God. They saw their children exhibit the same strength of faith as their parents and grandparents. They saw how their children made decisions in life through the lens of their faith and of their love for their spouses and their children. Love permeated their whole experience of family and life. It could truly be said of them that they lived and moved and had their being in union with God and each other. The love of God permeated their lives and the lives of their children.

Luke died at an old age, and he died in peace and joy. His wife was with him when he died, and she too was filled with peace and joy, notwithstanding that she would miss him. But each of their hearts was permeated with the knowledge of who they were, that they were beloved children of God, brother and sister of Christ, and in God's dwelling place, this would simply continue at a different and perfect level. Death was merely a door to that continued life that is eternal. Luke had lived a happy life, the kind of happy life that is nonexistent outside of communion with God and that is, indeed, the fruit of communion with God. Luke and his wife had participated in the very happiness of God.

# 6

## A STORY OF MISERY

Stuart was born and raised in a small town where conservative values held sway. Most of those in the town were churchgoers of one persuasion or another. Stuart's family was Catholic, and he went to the local Catholic grade school before going to the local public high school, there being no local Catholic high school. His parents would be described as lukewarm believers: they believed in God and in Jesus, but their belief had only a minor effect on their daily lives. They were not particularly prayerful, and they had no real evidence to give that God was in their lives on a daily basis. Stuart had absorbed this mentality, and he too had little real faith that affected his life.

Stuart was the youngest of three children. The other two were much older than him, and his mother would sometimes tell him that he was there "by mistake." He was actually very lonely, and he remained so throughout his growing-up years.

Stuart did okay at school but was not a scholar, nor was he a poor student. He did what was required to get him through. He was not a particularly friendly person, and as such, he had only one friend, and that was only to walk home from school with. Other than during the walk home, they never socialized together.

During the summer months, he would work on local farms. He had no particular direction to his life or any discernible great skills or talents that would lead toward a particular work goal or career direction.

When he finished high school, he left the small town to seek work in the big city. He rented a room and began a job search that ended with work in a nearby factory. The work was manual in nature and required no great training or aptitude. True to his nature, Stuart remained a loner, not developing friendships with anyone at work or in his neighborhood. Once he had moved away from home, he never attended church or in any way practiced what little faith he had. Even at this age and situation, Stuart never addressed the question of what he wanted out of life or what he wanted to do with his life. Life just happened each day, and Stuart just went along for the ride.

If you were to talk to Stuart for any length of time, you would soon discover he had no goals, no ambitions, nothing that would spark an effort in him in a particular direction. It would be difficult to pinpoint, from talking with him, why he was like this. He had no idea that life should be different or could be different. He seemed unaware that life could be deep and rich, that life was full of wonder and mystery and things that make living worthwhile.

He'd had a few dates with girls, but they soon found out this peculiar attribute about him: he simply wasn't an interesting person to be around. He simply didn't offer the hope that this was a person you'd want to make a life with. Even though he was lonely and getting lonelier, this fact didn't prompt him to want to improve his life. He was neither happy nor unhappy and seemed content to live like this.

When he was approaching thirty years of age, he was involved in a minor accident that left him with a neck injury. As time went on, the injury didn't seem to resolve itself. He found that it affected his ability to do his job and told his boss that he was having difficulty because of the injury. His boss told him they didn't have another position for him and recommended therapy. He obtained the therapy but it didn't help him either. He didn't realize that the neck injury wasn't the problem.

As time passed, he went for further checkups and discovered he had a cancer in the neck area that was becoming intertwined with his spine. He was told that they could operate but that the operation was very risky and that he could be left with permanent spinal damage that could leave him unable to move his neck. They told him that other treatments would be unlikely to get rid of the cancer, so the risky surgery was his only real option.

Stuart had the operation, and it left him exactly as they had predicted, except that they hadn't predicted the pain he would be left with. Stuart was left unable to lift his head, so that he was permanently left looking at the ground, and he was in constant pain because of residual scar tissue that placed pressure on his spine. He was told that no further treatment was possible for him, and the best they could offer him was a brace that helped reduce some of the pressure on the spine.

Stuart was unable to continue in his job, but the company was able to find another position for him that hopefully would minimize the strain on his neck. He learned the job, but as time went on, he found that even this reduced but constant strain on his neck was producing intolerable pain that could only be partially helped with pain-killing drugs.

When he went to bed at night, he found his neck made it difficult for him to sleep. After about a year, Stuart was in constant pain and sleep deprivation. He was lonelier than ever, and it began to dawn on him that this was going to be his life. Slowly, as the significance of what this meant came to him, he entered into a depression, which saw him trapped inside this body that was forever going to be a source of pain and disability. He had no real friends to talk to to share his despondency with or commiserate with, and he had no God to talk to who could offer him spiritual hope. He went to work each day, suffered through the day, and then returned home to a lonely evening and a night of restless sleep. He had only minimal contact with his family, and they weren't able to offer much empathy or help for him.

One day, Stuart was at work when he felt extremely sharp pain spasms coming from his neck. They were so painful he doubled over and was unable to continue his work. He was sent to the emergency room at the local hospital. A coworker stayed with him while he awaited examination. The examination indicated that it was possible that the cancer had returned, and Stuart was admitted for tests. The tests revealed that the cancer had indeed returned and that the prognosis for Stuart was very bleak. He was told that an operation would be impossible. The only treatment available was chemotherapy, and they told him that this was unlikely to eliminate the cancer. The cancer was a slow-growing type, and they hoped that it might be reduced in size so that he could live somewhat longer. Nonetheless, the best they said he could hope for was perhaps two more years of life.

Stuart took the chemotherapy, and it did reduce the size of the tumor to the point that the excruciating pain was somewhat relieved. He was sent to a rehabilitation center during the period of his treatment, and then he was released to go home. He had arranged to take leave from work and return to his family.

Even during this time, Stuart never sought the consolation of faith, never saw a priest or asked for the Sacrament of the Sick. He never received the consolation of having a dear friend who would share this part of his life with him. And he never received any hope that doctors could do anything to make the remainder of his life more comfortable. He had returned home so that he could recover from the chemotherapy and hopefully have someone around who might be able to help him through this period. He had told his family what his medical condition and outlook were. By this time, his parents were old and frail, and he wasn't sure how much they would be able to help him. Still, they welcomed him and told him they would do whatever they could for him. Their family doctor had said he would do the same.

Stuart found that he could ease his pain somewhat if he propped his head at a certain angle while lying down, but he could do this for only limited periods of time. The result was that he was tormented almost continuously by a pain that was like a migraine headache in intensity, accompanied by shooting pains at regular intervals.

One day his mother came to sit with him, asking if there was anything at all that she could do to help. He said she had done all she could and that he was just thankful to be home, to be with someone who cared for him during this time, and that he wasn't alone.

It was during this conversation that he said to her, "Mom, I feel like I haven't had a life, and here I am dying. I feel like I've never done anything worthwhile in my life or done things most other people have done. I feel like I've been alone and left out, and now here I am with a disease that tells me I've only got so long left, and that I'll never be able to do what others do normally. I don't know why it is that I've never seemed to be interested in doing what other people do. I never seemed to have a goal in life to strive toward, and I've never had any luck with women, so the idea of love and family never seemed to have been a possibility for me. I've never had much belief in God, so even God hasn't been much of a factor in my life. And now that I'm dying, isn't it hypocritical of me to turn to God for help? Do you think I should ask Fr. John to come and see me?"

"Son," she answered, "none of us in this family has had ambition for really important things in our lives. Your father and I just sort of fell in together. There was never a huge love affair or desire for family that we told each other about. Everything just sort of happened. We didn't have any plans or goals. Life just went on, willy-nilly, and

I think you just carried on the way we did. It's too bad you never met someone and had the chance at a family, but when I look at your father and me, it was just luck we met and married. Sometimes I even think that we just did what was expected of us at the time. That's what couples did—got married and had kids. I can't say that we had any more reason than that. The way I see it, you just never met the right person. As to getting right with God, I think you need to do this. You don't want to risk not being with God when your time comes. Do you want me to ask Fr. John to come and see you?"

"Yes, please," he answered. "I hope he'll see me."

Fr. John came to see Stuart that evening and the two spent a long time together. At one point, Stuart said to Fr. John, "Father, I was telling my mother today how I feel like I've never had a life. I've always felt alone, always felt left out, always felt my life had no real value, and always felt that I never had any particular talents that were worthwhile. I always felt that I was just a blah person with a blah life and this was how life would always be. I don't know why I felt this way, and I felt that I was trapped in this blah-ness and that there was nothing I could do about it. So I just passed time each day, and I haven't really done anything with my life. I feel like I have wasted my life, and I feel sorry about that.

"But even when I say this, I don't know what I would have done or could have done to change it. I feel like my life was just a low-level sort of misery to be endured until it was over. To tell you the truth, as much as I feel sad that I'm now dying, in a way it's a relief because my life really wasn't worth living. Father, I feel like this is some sort of sin, and that I need to tell God that I'm sorry I wasted the life he gave me. I don't want to be separated from him forever, and I want to do whatever I can now to be made right with him. Please forgive me my sins and tell me what I can do during the rest of my life to come closer to God."

"Stuart," Fr. John began, "I'm glad that you came home to your family at this time, and I'm glad that you are seeking to come home to your Father in heaven. The wonderful thing about God is that he always welcomes home those who wish to return to him. It's not so important what the reason for that is. Imagine if we couldn't come back to God just because circumstances almost force us to. I'm glad, and I'm certain God is glad, that you know enough to turn back to him, especially at this time when you are only a short time away from seeing him face to face.

"I'm glad, too, that you are thinking about your life and how you have led it. The same thing I said about God is true about life. We have the wonderful ability to begin anew at any point in our lives, so tonight you have done two things well: you have sought to renew your life with God, and you have, in effect, taken a step to begin your life anew. You have come to God with contrition in your heart for not living your life as best you could, and God forgives you your sins. Now you have a chance to live your life anew, with a clean slate, and I will help you as best I can to live your life anew with God.

"Stuart, living life with God is actually quite simple to understand, although sometimes we find it difficult to do this. Just remember that God is always near, as near as a glance in his direction. You live with God when you decide to live with God. You speak with God when you decide to speak with God. You listen to God when you decide to read or hear his words. These are all things that simply need our decision to begin and then our effort at doing. You don't have to come to me to begin your life with God. You do that when you decide to do it and begin doing it.

"I want you to know something about God that is helpful in getting our attitude toward him right. God is a happy fellow. This may sound strange, because we so often have an image of God who is trying to catch us for our wrongdoing, but the truth is that God made us for himself so that we can share in his life now and forever. Think of God as the one who truly knows you and loves you, and who wants you to be his child in spirit and truth. Stuart, just think of what that means, that God is your Father. Begin to talk to him each day as your Father. Try to picture him as the one who is rejoicing at your return to him, who is filled with joy that you are back with him, and who wants you now to share in his love and joy. Have this image of God and it will make it easier for you to want to be his, and to be in his presence each day. Know that he is with you each moment. Place everything his hands, and let him take care of the rest."

The next morning, Fr. John explained to Stuart the Sacrament of the Sick, anointed him, and then gave him communion. Fr. John brought two books for Stuart: a book of daily prayer and a book of reflections on God, which reflected on God the Father, the Son, and the Holy Spirit.

From the first book, Stuart began to learn how to pray each day, and from the second, Stuart began to know who God is and how to think about each of the Persons of the Trinity. Stuart began to know that Jesus was with him each moment.

After the Sacrament of the Sick, Stuart was left with a deep peace in his heart and a desire to love God more. These were the gifts that God gave him through this anointing. Stuart began to actually feel the joy of being a son of God, and what it meant to be an heir. The more Stuart read of God and actually prayed each day, the more he was filled with peace, and a joy began to emerge in his heart.

One day his mother came to sit with him and she said to him, "Stuart, you look happy. Even with what is happening to you and the pain you are in, you look happy. Even seeing this in you makes me happy, too. Can you tell me about this happiness you seem to have so abundantly?"

"Sure, Mom," he said. "It's because I *am* happy. For the first time in my life, I have peace in my heart and good thoughts in my mind. I am actually looking forward to something for the first time in my life. Can you imagine? I'm actually looking forward to being with God, not because I want this life to end but because I have learned so much about who God is and what kind of God he is. Imagine, Mom, being with someone forever who is filled with love and joy and goodness and who wants to share that life with you. I know now that God loves me; I can *feel* his love for me. And I don't know how he brings this about, but I actually feel love for God.

"Mom, I have not felt love for anyone in my whole life the way I feel love for God now. Isn't that a miracle? That's why I'm so happy now. And even this pain I have is not so painful anymore. I know God knows my pain, but I also know he is with me each moment sharing in it. But this is only for a while. My life with him, which only began the night Fr. John came to see me, is forever. So it's not so bad, knowing this pain is for a short time only, but my life with God is forever. I am happy, Mom, as happy as anyone could be."

# 7

# A STORY OF SEPARATION

In a small town north of Toronto, two brothers worked a farm they co-owned and had a business repairing farm equipment. Each brother had a small family, and each family was well known in the area. They were humble people who were liked by their neighbors. They had a good repair business based on their reputation for honesty, good workmanship, and fair dealing.

The brothers were part of a larger family of eight siblings, all of whom lived in the area. The entire family had been in the area now for four generations. They were Catholic by heritage and daily belief. Their children went to local Catholic schools. The families met regularly for family celebrations and events. They were seen as a close-knit family who could be counted on for support from one another. They were seen as a family that loved one another and could be relied on for help whenever help was needed.

One friend of the family put it simply when describing the family: "Salt of the earth, solid citizens. Anyone would want to be their friend."

The family was never wealthy and, for the most part, struggled financially over the years as the farm produced a subsistence type of income. Just when they were getting ahead, a crop failure would set them back again. Each of the family members who were involved in farming had to supplement their incomes from other sources. Some worked at other jobs during the winter and sometimes even during the summer.

Some invested, as the two brothers did, in a business they owned and operated. All the members of the family were concerned for the next generation because there were none that expressed any interest in carrying on the farming business. Most wanted to attend university and obtain good careers in the cities. Some wanted to be teachers, others wanted to get into the medical field in one way or another, and two wanted to enter the business world. None wanted to stay in this small community that was so dependent on farming.

It happened that one of the brothers, Bernie, had an uncle by marriage that lived in California who was involved in the wine business and had large vineyards. He needed good help and asked Bernie if he would consider relocating to California on a permanent basis to manage two of the vineyards. The proposition was very attractive financially, and the location of the vineyards in California offered more assurance of annual crop production because of the climate and types of rainfall each year. The crop season was longer and more predictable than they had ever experienced in their present location. From a business and future point of view, the move made sense.

But making the decision to move, from a family point of view, was excruciating. Bernie was very close to his siblings and his parents, and so too was he to his wife's family, who also were a farming family in the area. To this point, none of the family had moved away. All they had ever known was closeness in family ties and presence to one another.

Bernie had discussed the offer with all of them and one night they had decided to come together to discuss the ramifications of such a move. It was typical of the family that they began with a prayer that God would guide them all in their decision making.

Bernie's three daughters were particularly alarmed at the possibility of a move. Even though they did not want to continue in the farming tradition, it never occurred to them to move any distance from their family. The love that was in the family was too important to them, and they wanted to raise their own families in this way, with all the members close in both proximity and relationship to each other. One by one, each of the siblings spoke in favor of or against the move, stating very clearly their reasons.

Before the parents spoke, the key "pro" thoughts given were summarized as: it was a good and generous offer, providing Bernie and his family with a future and a means to provide education to the girls; it was good for Bernie as a farmer because his knowledge and experience would be a great assist to the uncle in California; they would still be part of a family-run operation, so that family values could still be a key part of their way of life.

The "con" thoughts were these: their move would break up the family; it would leave the remaining brother financially at risk; finally, the move was just too difficult emotionally for the family to bear—what could be more important than keeping the family together? This was a move that was going to change the future of the whole family.

Bernie's parent's-in-law spoke next and advised that Bernie and his wife's first responsibility was to provide a future for themselves and their family, and that no matter how difficult the move, they should make their decision with that priority in mind.

Bernie's parents advised that whatever they did, they should do it as a consequence of prayer and good sense, and that they should not let the emotional difficulty of the decision dictate their final decision. No matter what they decided, his parents said they would be behind it in whatever way they could help.

With all this input, Bernie and his wife and three girls returned to their home to discuss the matter further. In the end, the three girls told their father that they agreed with what their grandparents had said and that they would willingly go with whatever their parents decided. They said they knew they would make the right decision through prayer and careful thought.

So it was that Bernie and his wife decided that night that moving to California was the best thing for them to do. The next day, they told everyone their decision, and it was decided that Bernie would leave for California the next week and the family would follow at the end of the school year.

And so it went. Before the move, a large going away party was held. All their friends and family were there. There were tears and hugs and best wishes and small going-away gifts. Then came the actual moving day, final goodbyes, and flight to California.

After they left, the rest of the family went into a period of mourning. They missed the five of them terribly. The girls' grandparents grieved the loss of knowing their future great-grandchildren. The siblings and their spouses missed their brother and sister-in-law, and sister and brother-in-law, and their children.

Andy, the remaining brother, particularly missed his brother who had been such a friend and confidant and partner in life for most of their lives. Another brother had decided to join with Andy in the operation of the farm and in the repair business. After a year, they all had adjusted to the loss of their family members and to the business repercussions of the move. Even so, a large hole had come into the fabric of the family, and this was likely never to be closed.

In the meantime, Bernie and his family were adjusting to their changed circumstances. Bernie found the wine business very satisfying as a farming enterprise. He found he had no difficulty making the switch to this type of crop and in coming to know what created the best conditions for the crop and its harvesting. Financially, he was, for the first time in his life, feeling that he had security in which he could actually make firm plans for the future. He had even discussed with the girls how he could help them attend university.

His wife was beginning to make the adjustments in her life. She made friends with her great-uncle's family, with other people who worked the vineyards, and with neighbors. Especially helpful were the people they met at their new parish. The girls, too, were making their adjustments, meeting girls at the parish and at their school.

After a year, each member of the family had made the adjustment to their new way of life. Each of them still missed their family back home, and none of them as yet thought of California as home. They all knew the move was in the best interest of the family from a business and financial point of view, but they all had a hole in their heart that their larger family back home filled. And none of them thought this would ever be healed.

Bernie had been concerned all along with how his wife would adjust to the move. Would she be able to be happy in California? Would she be able to live permanently away from her roots, from the love she had known in her family? Would she be able to stick to their decision if she felt that the loss of family was just too great a price to pay for financial security? He frankly didn't think she would be able to make the turn, and he was totally prepared to move back home if she indicated she couldn't be happy away from them.

He was concerned for the girls as well, although less so, because he felt they were at an age when they could adapt better than he and his wife could. And he felt that if his wife did acquire happiness in California, they would as well because she had such a positive influence in their lives.

In the meantime, their faith would help them make the transition, he reasoned, because he, and they, believed that the Lord was with them in this venture that made them the first to "leave home." The decision had finally been made in prayer, and in the belief the Lord was leading them to their new home.

It was this last element that was decisive for his wife. She had certainty that their decision was the right decision because of the sense she had attained through prayer that the Lord himself was leading them away from their origins to a new land. She felt like Abram being led to a place he didn't know.[6] She even felt kindred to him in the sense of God making Abram father to a whole nation.[7] She felt that this would happen when her girls married and began their own families in this new place, and this would make California their home forever, where their grandchildren and great-grandchildren would live and raise their families.

Such were her thoughts even before they made the move. Such was the strength of her conviction that God had provided this opportunity for them. Far more than Bernie, she had a sense of destiny in the move led by God. And so it was that she had an inner peace about the move that was unshakable.

After five years, the girls themselves had finished high school and gone on to college, so that each of them was away during the college years. Each of them grew as young

---

6      Genesis 12:1
7      Genesis 12:2

women through this time away and became people who knew themselves and developed a high sense of what they wanted for their lives.

They told their parents that they would like to live in the vineyard area because they loved the country so much and because they didn't want to move far from their parents. But they would be living in the cities nearby where they could undertake their chosen careers. One of them had met the man, who was from the area, she would eventually marry. Indeed, two years after she graduated, they married and settled down in his hometown. Each of the other two began their careers in that city, so that the three of them remained in close proximity. One of them also married, and the other remained single.

Soon there were grandchildren, cementing the mother's vision of life in California as being irreversible. Bernie saw her confidence in the move and soon forgot his concerns about her ability to adjust to their new home. He was making enough money to help the girls go to college and to allow them to visit their family back home each summer. And various members of the family would come west to visit them.

After ten years, all had adjusted to the new life, both Bernie's family and the families back home. Indeed, the children of his siblings all did as they had said they would. They all left the farm community and moved to cities where they settled down. This was the new reality, and while there was some nostalgia for the "good old days," life went on in the new paradigm, and love still held the families close in spirit.

Twenty-five years later, Bernie was ready to retire, and the two married girls had had seven children, the eldest of whom were now graduating themselves, and one was now married. These children knew little of the family "back home." Bernie's wife was happy that the girls had remained geographically close to them, so they were together frequently, and the three girls remained close to each other in relationship.

Bernie and his wife were very involved in their parish and had been for years. They saw that their girls and their children had faith, and this was a great source of joy to them. The move to California had been a great success in every way they could think of, and they were grateful to God for having had the opportunity to make such a move.

Life "back home" had carried on as well, except that the farming life became less and less of a feature in the ways of making a living by most of Bernie and his wife's siblings. Only one now had a farm, and he had still to supplement his income to make a go of it. All the others had sold their farms and taken up other means of earning a living. They had all adjusted to their new realities. Even through the changes, which for some were traumatic, their faith remained intact, and most of the children retained their faith.

The separation of Bernie and his family from the rest had proven good for them, had been one that was undertaken in faith, had the result of building each one in his or her faith, and had changed the whole future of their family. They went with apprehension but with faith in God, and he had kept them in his care through the years. God was good and was seen to be good.

# 8

# A STORY OF REUNION

After Bernie retired, they continued to live in the home they had on the vineyard. He still helped out with certain aspects of the vineyard, but this was more in the way of assisting those who had taken over its management from him. He had time to do some other things that were of interest to him, but as time went on, he felt he wanted to reconnect with his siblings back in the Toronto area. Most of them were now retired or nearing retirement, and Bernie felt he wanted to find a way to be able to spend enough time with them so as to re-establish the close bond they had when they all lived in the same community.

He spoke of this desire with his wife, and she too had some of those yearnings. They talked about it often and discussed various options they might have in how to go about it.

They didn't want to move back to Ontario from California because their children were all there. They considered the possibility of a series of visits over a period of time. They thought about an extended stay during the summer months. They thought about the possibility of staying for brief periods with certain of their siblings. They considered buying a vehicle in which they could both travel and live while they made their visit.

During these discussions, they were concerned about becoming a burden on anyone they visited and overstaying their welcome. They considered having all the family come to California for a reunion, where they would visit various parts of California together. In the end, they thought this would be too expensive and impractical.

After many discussions, they weren't sure what they would do. They decided they didn't know what the actual goal was of their desires. They decided that they needed to know what it was they were trying to accomplish, and then, once knowing that, maybe it would be easier for them to decide on the means of accomplishing the goal. In the meantime, they had hinted at what they were thinking about with their daughters and found that the girls had similar longings.

Each of them, it was found from discussion, had a longing to be reconnected with their families. They wanted to know how each member of the family was doing, what their hopes were, what their problems were, what their state of happiness was. They knew they couldn't do this with a quick visit, but they couldn't think of a practical way of doing it.

"I have a thought," said one of the daughters. "Why don't we arrange for a three-day reunion at some hotel or facility in the area, where we could format a way of coming together that would allow all of us to get to know each other again. Maybe there could be periods of specific kinds of sharing between us that would help us reconnect. I could see such an event going a long way in a short time to achieve what we seem to want."

The idea was greeted with enthusiasm, and they all started thinking about how such a weekend could be structured and facilitated. After many discussions, they decided they didn't want the event to be simply a walk down memory lane, nor a time for brief visits or trips around the area. They wanted something that would be of lasting benefit to everyone who was there, accomplished through something that wouldn't take much time, and that would have the chance to really get them in touch with one another and to renew in a deeper way their love for one another.

The eldest girl once again came through with the central idea. "You know that every time something significant has happened with us, it has always involved Jesus in some way or another. He always takes care of us. And each of us knows from retreats and other things how he brings about what he wants for us if we give him a chance, if we put him first, and if we make him the focal point. So why don't we do that now? Why don't we provide a kind of retreat-type setting that allows us to all be in the same place, having our own places to sleep, having all our meals together, having Mass each day, and providing times when a talk could be given to focus our attention and sharing. I think such a weekend could be the deeper coming together that we all long for."

They thought it was a great idea, and Bernie called two of his brothers to bounce the idea off them and to ask them to get others' thoughts on it. They responded with enthusiasm to the idea, and one of them had even checked with a local retreat center to see if the family could occupy the center for a weekend, arriving on a Thursday evening and leaving on a Sunday after lunch. They would all stay there for the weekend.

One of the brothers spoke to the spiritual director of the center to tell him what had been discussed, and he too became enthusiastic about the idea. He had known members of the family for many years and knew of the faith level that existed throughout the family. He asked if he could put together some ideas for a retreat around which the whole enterprise could function. He felt certain that something could be put together that would be extremely rich for the whole family and that would accomplish all of their desired objectives.

He did so, and finally, after much emailing and further thoughts, plans were made for the event to take place the following June. Most of the family was committed to the reunion and excited about the way it was being done. All had seen the spiritual director's program and agreed it had the ingredients for a fantastic time together and a time together with the Lord. Many thought this might just be the most important family time ever, with fruits they could only hope for and guess at. They even had a theme for the reunion: *Together again in Christ. Praise be to God.*

The parents of Bernie and his wife had died a few years earlier, but there were parents of some of the spouses who were still alive and who wanted to come to the reunion. In total, there were eight of these, sixteen of Bernie and his siblings and their spouses, thirty-two children and their spouses, fifty-eight grandchildren, including some spouses, and ten great-grandchildren. Arrangements had been made that all the great-grandchildren would be taken care of during the retreat but would not be present during the activities. All of the grandchildren were old enough to participate in the retreat. There were only five people who weren't able to make the reunion, and three of these were because they had offered to take care of the great-grandchildren during the retreat. In total, there were 109 attending the retreat for the full three days. People from every age group, except the very young, were included.

All those who were coming from any distance were being put up in various family members' homes in the area. They were to arrive three days before the retreat so that they could get to spend some time with family members and do some sightseeing, and they were to stay for a further two days after the retreat.

When the time came, all arrived as scheduled, and everybody had a chance to meet each other before the retreat. They caught up on news, met family members they had never met before, had a chance to meet some old friends and to see certain points of interest in the Toronto area that they had not seen before or wanted especially to see again after so many years. By the time of the retreat, everyone was relaxed and looking forward to what would take place over the next three days. Some had a bit of anxiety that three days wouldn't be enough time for everyone to get to know each other in the way they hoped when the planning was taking place.

On the Thursday evening, after all had assembled and checked into their rooms, Fr. Norm, the spiritual director, welcomed them to the retreat center and told them he was privileged to be part of such a unique family reunion. He had never seen such a thing before, where a family had chosen a retreat format as the means of coming together after so many years, and he thought the Lord would reward them abundantly over the three days for having done so. He asked everyone, young and old and in between, to enjoy the time together, and the best way they could do that would be to fully participate in the exercises. He said he felt certain the exercises decided on would fulfill all their hopes for the weekend.

He then led a meditation intended to set the tone for the weekend and to get it off on the right foot. The meditation combined two themes: "Who is God?" and "Who are you?" In the talk, Fr. Norm spoke about the nature of God in the sense of the kind of God that God is, and stressed the loving and giving nature of God, and this led naturally into why God made each of us. He started by giving the old Baltimore Catechism answer to the question, why did God make us? Most there were able to give the answer: to know, love, and serve God in this world and to be forever happy with him in the next. He then spoke of the need to get to know who we are in the context of this answer, and he said that Friday would be spent for the most part exploring the question of who each person is.

When Friday came, all the participants were placed at tables of eight. It was arranged that each table was comprised of members of different families with a mixture of every age group and gender.

The day began with one of the younger members of the family giving a prepared history of herself and telling of what her hopes were for herself and for the family. After this short talk, each person at the table was invited to give a brief and similar statement about himself or herself.

Fr. Norm followed this by giving a spiritual direction on the meaning of the person. In this talk, Fr. Norm spoke of the irreplaceable uniqueness of each person in terms of personality, giftedness, and ability to love and be loved. He spoke of the roles of persons as grandparent, parent, son or daughter, sibling, married, or single. He spoke, as well, of the hopes each person created in the heart and mind of their parents when they were born and through their formative years. He then asked everyone to share at their tables what each thought was the most important characteristic of each of the other persons at their table.

After this, there was time provided for the tables to continue their discussions with one another, and then, just before Mass, one of the musicians among the family members played violin for all to enjoy. At the Mass, different members of the family formed a choir to lead the singing; others read the readings and brought forward the gifts.

Father's homily continued the theme of the value of the person, but this time he linked it to Jesus' talk to the rich young man who asked Jesus what he must do to inherit eternal life.[8] He told them what a fortunate family they were and how exceptional in this regard they were from his experience with families of today. He told them what a privilege it was to see a family that did as Jesus asked of them, and that was to follow him. He said that as the weekend went on, he wanted to come back to this thought about what it meant to be followers of Jesus in this day and age. He added that he wanted to share with them his

---

8    Luke 18:18–23

thoughts on what he thought faith had meant to them in terms of their happiness and love.

At lunch, all were asked to sit with someone they didn't know very well so that they might have an opportunity to meet more of the family as the weekend passed. A break period was given after lunch for a rest or walk, and then the group reconvened for an afternoon that comprised two further talks. The first was given by Bernie, who spoke of what it had meant for them to have left home for California, and he told what California had brought them, of the growth in the family, of what life was like in that part of the United States, and of what the church was like in that part of the world. Each was asked to share with the others how they decided on their direction in life and how that direction had worked out for them.

Fr. Norm then followed up with a talk on Abram's leaving his family and friends to follow God's will for him to move to a strange land God would show him.[9] "Isn't this the case of each person?" Fr. Norm asked. "Haven't each of us here had to answer this call, whatever it entailed, to go where God would show them? And hasn't this been accompanied by some apprehension on what this might mean to us? For many here, it meant moving to another place to follow that leading of the heart that somehow gave us direction in life, and in the end, for those who know God and his ways, we find that very impulse is from him. Share with each other how God has led you to the life you have led."

And so young and old alike shared on this point, how God had led them in their lives. After this was over, Fr. Norm said, "I think we see two things from this sharing:

---

9   Genesis 12:1

the first is that God is in our lives so intimately that he knows who we are and that his leading in our lives is totally in harmony with who we are as persons. This is how God not only shows his presence in our lives, but how he loves each of us individually."

After this, one person from each table was asked to share how God had led them in their lives. From oldest to youngest, each was able to share clearly how God had led them in their life's journey. And all were inspired by how personally God had acted with each person and how he had cared for each of them.

On the Friday night, different family members provided an evening of skits and music. By the end of Friday, there was a feeling of love and gladness permeating the entire family that such an event had been planned and brought about.

The focus of Saturday shifted away from each person. Fr. Norm said, "Remember what I said at the beginning of this time together? We want to get to know ourselves, and we want to get to know God. Today we want to move our focus to Jesus and see what he shows us about God and about ourselves. I want to begin the day with a meditation on Jesus."

Fr. Norm then went on to recite the Scripture account of Jesus calling Peter and Andrew to follow him.[10] "It may seem strange that I begin this day focusing on Jesus' call to two people to follow him. But here is a message that I think will set the stage for a wonderful day together. Jesus told Peter and Andrew, 'Follow me and I will make you fishers of men.' Jesus says to each of us, 'Follow me and I

---

10   Matthew 4:18–20

will make you ...' This is what I want to focus on: what has Jesus called each of us to be in our lives? He asked them to consider that question and to write down their answers.

A member of the family then gave a talk on this question. He said that he had known for much of his life that Jesus was in his life. He had learned that from his parents, and he saw how much they loved Jesus and how important Jesus was in their lives. "How many times did they tell me that Jesus loved me and that Jesus would help me become the person he wanted me to be if I but gave him a chance? Like most of us here, I think, I wanted to live by faith and to be a person formed by faith. If I did that, I reasoned, Jesus would take care of the rest in terms of leading me in life but also in terms of developing me as a person. I had seen that he had done that with my parents, and I wanted to have a character like they had.

"You all know me well enough to know if I'm telling the truth or not or if I see myself rightly or not. Here is what I think Jesus has done with me. To get to this picture, I've had to ask others who know me well to help me out because I don't really say that I know myself as well as I'm going to tell.

"I believe that I am a loving person. If I am, it's because I've seen the love of my parents, and I've seen the love within this family. Jesus said, 'Love one another as I have loved you,'[11] and I have seen the love that this family is capable of, the sacrifice that this family is capable of, and how the love that Jesus has is displayed in this family. I hope that I, too, love like this. This is how I want to love. This is what I want to be as a person. And I ask Jesus to help me to be this person."

---

11   John 15:12

*Happiness Is*

This was the essence of what he had to say. The question given for sharing at the tables was this: "What do you think Jesus has made you?" After the sharing at tables, Mass was celebrated, followed by lunch.

In the afternoon, Fr. Norm gave a reflection on Jesus as the visible image of the love of God. In it, he spoke of the faithfulness of Jesus to the Father's will, his understanding of it, and his understanding of the will of God for all people to be in communion with him. He spoke of Jesus' humanness and of his willingness to speak of God to all and to heal all who came to him and to go out to those who were separated from God.

When he had said these things, he asked one of Bernie's brothers to come and speak on how God had been experienced in the family as he had known it.

Bernie's brother spoke of the times when God had seen them through tough times and crises of health and how they had known God's faithfulness to them when crops had failed and things looked the bleakest. He spoke of Bernie's leaving and the hole in the family that created and how God had helped them to see that he had brought everyone through to a new understanding of his mysterious ways. He spoke of the birth of their children and the awe and thanksgiving this gave them toward God. He spoke of how their parents had died and how they were so at peace during the final days and hours and how their deaths had affected everyone who had been with them. Everyone was certain they were now with God, in the very presence of God, and how they, too, looked forward to that future in heaven where all would be together again in the very presence of God.

When he had finished, he asked everyone to share at their tables of how they had experienced God in the family and of their hopes for the future with God.

The sharing was deep and powerful as one after another spoke of how they had experienced God so constantly in their lives, sharing particular times when God made himself so visible to them. When the sharing had ended, there was such a joy in the room that it led to spontaneous singing in praise of God. From old to young, there was a participation in something that was bigger than any of them individually, something that transcended their own understanding of God and life with him.

For supper and the evening activities, the three who had been taking care of the children came with the children to join them. On that evening, there was a barbeque outside followed by a time of simply being together and getting caught up with particular people each wanted to see and spend time with. Some went to bed very late that night as they got caught up in their conversations.

On the Sunday morning, Fr. Norm gave a reflection on the role of the Christian family in the world in which we live. He spoke with eloquence of the very nature of love that existed and was created in the family where Christ was central. He spoke of this family before him and saw in them everything that was proclaimed about the family by the church. He saw in them the very process by which God permeated a couple's love and in whose love new persons were created in the image of God, new persons destined to live their lives with God in this life and the next. "What a hope that represents for all who know you," he said.

*Happiness Is*

Before Mass, he asked those at the tables to share on one last subject. "What have you received from God this weekend? What key thing will you take away from this time together and with God?" Again, the sharing was deep and profound. After this, the whole family, including the babysitters and the babysat, joined in the final Eucharist. The weekend concluded with lunch. After some further time together all returned to their homes.

Bernie and his family returned to California filled with such joy at what had transpired. No one felt that there was anything that went unsaid or undone. The feeling of Christ's presence among them was palpable, and the sense of the fullness of love was pervasive throughout the weekend.

Bernie said to his wife, the night they returned to their home, "I can't imagine that there could be a greater happiness than what we have just experienced, short of being in heaven itself. I can't imagine that more love and caring could exist in our family. And it doesn't matter at all where people are in terms of physical proximity to one another. Christ has given all the love we could hope for and all the reason for living fully that one could have. I saw real happiness over the last weekend, a real state of heart and spirit that is never going to end. Thanks be to God for the life he has given us."

# 9

# HOLINESS AND HAPPINESS

Holiness and happiness are linked, and the stories thus far have served to hint at the linkage. It may be thought that the stories show a simplistic view of life with God in that they show a constant thread of peace of heart that comes with life in God, with God, and through God.

In spite of his suffering, Jesus' heart was at peace. At the Last Supper, Jesus said, "Peace I bequeath to you, my own peace I give you, a peace the world cannot give, this is my gift to you. Do not let your hearts be troubled or afraid."[12] After he rose, "the disciples were filled with joy, and he said to them, 'Peace be with you.'"[13] And then he

---

12   John 14:27
13   John 20:20–21

said, "As the Father sent me, so am I sending you."[14] Here is the link between holiness and happiness: being part of the Father's life and will and the peace of heart that flows from it.

To look into this further, we need to look at the peace of heart that Jesus had, and that *he* bequeaths to us when we are in him. It comes in the same way as everything else comes from him and through him. "I am the vine, you are the branches. Whoever remains in me, with me in him, bears fruit in plenty; for cut off from me you can do nothing. It is to the glory of the Father that you should bear much fruit, and then you will be my disciples. Remain in my love. If you keep my commandments you will remain in my love, just as I have kept my Father's commandments and remain in his love. I have told you this so that my own joy may be in you and your joy may be complete. This is my commandment: love one another as I have loved you."[15]

Being in Jesus, being with Jesus, leads to taking on the same heart and mind as him, having his peace and joy, his happiness. Holiness is in God alone, and is in Jesus. Holiness is having that heart and mind that is in Jesus and that comes from the Father's will for us. Indeed, it comes from the very same happiness that is in God by his very nature. Let us look further at the nature of holiness and the nature of happiness to see how completely interlinked they are.

God alone is holy. To understand holiness is to look at God and see what he is in his very nature. To do this, we need only to look at Jesus, who is the visible image of

---

14  John 20:21
15  John 15:5, 8–12

God. Jesus is God and man, and in him we see the nature of the Father.

"'I am the Way, the Truth and the Life. No one can come to the Father except through me. If you know me, you know my Father too. From this moment you know him and have seen him.'

"Philip said, 'Lord, let us see the Father and then we shall be satisfied.'

"'Have I been with you all this time, Philip,' Jesus said to him, 'and you still do not know me? To have seen me is to have seen the Father. The words I say to you I do not speak as from myself: it is the Father, living in me, who is doing this work. You must believe me when I say that I am in the Father and the Father is in me.'"[16]

Holiness is characterized by three factors: goodness, love, and self-giving. When we look at each of these, we come to a better idea that holiness is an active thing, not a passive thing. It involves a state of being that is not only something, but is doing something. The *being* and the *doing* are totally interrelated. For example, my state of being affects what I do and how I do it. If I am selfish at the very core of my being, my doing will be selfish. If I am caring about others at the very core of my being, my doing will express this caring for others. From what Jesus *does*, we can see what his *being* is, and from this we can see what constitutes his holiness.

Goodness can be described as that state of being that is good, is beneficial to others, and that produces thoughts and actions that are beneficial to others. It is a state of

---

16   John 14:6–11

being that sees the needs of others and acts accordingly. When we see that Jesus restored life to the son of the widow of Nain,[17] we see that he did something good for her, something that brought her happiness and relief: it was something that came from Jesus' compassion for her plight. When we see Jesus healing the lepers,[18] we see his goodness displayed because of his understanding of their situation as outcasts in society and his compassion for their suffering. We see in these actions of Jesus a heart of compassion and a mind that understood the plight of people. His actions are signs of goodness that is in his very being. All of his actions in healing people came from this goodness at the core of his being. This same goodness is in the Father. Jesus is the visible image of the Father, and in his actions, Jesus reveals the goodness that is in him and in the Father.

Love can be described as many things, but for our purposes here, love is defined as that attribute in a person that cares about another. Love is characterized by caring for another. A person who is loved knows he or she is loved by the caring he or she sees and feels from the caring one. One feels loved by the one who loves him or her. The love may be characterized by some statement or action taken by the person, but what is communicated to the loved one is that the person really cares about him or her. He or she has the sense that the person understands who the other is and cares about him or her. It is personal and intimate in nature, and it affects the person being loved.

When we look at Jesus' love for his disciples, what was it that most characterized that love? Look at what Jesus

---

17  Luke 7:11–17
18  Luke 17:12

did. He gathered his disciples around himself. He created friendship with them. They came to know him, and they came to know that he knew each of them. Jesus was not a leader "from afar" but was a leader who knew his flock and whose flock knew him. Even more, Jesus knew his flock, each and every one, in the most intimate way one can know someone because he understood human nature, the wonder of the human person, and the desire of God to be in relationship with man and man with God.

He called each of them, he explained himself to them repeatedly, he showed them again and again who he was by the things he said and did, and he corrected them when they needed correction. All the while, he was building them up for the time they themselves would carry on his work, proclaim the kingdom of God as he did, and be faithful to God just as he was faithful. He had, in the end, replicated his mind and heart in them in ways where they, too, loved others as he did. And this was because they had seen in Jesus the very nature of the love of God that was now part of their very beings.

Nothing so displays the love of God than the act of giving of self that was so displayed in the life of Jesus. Here we see the "outward face" of love, the action that flows from the heart that cares, from the mind that understands need, and from a spirit that is free to give. Whether it was in the way he went among the people proclaiming that the kingdom of God was near, the way he gathered people around himself to whom he was committed, the way he reached out to the outcasts of society, the way he confronted the hypocrisy in many of the religious leaders of the day, or the way he gave his life at the end for the benefit of us all, Jesus was a person who gave all of himself for others, who understood what it meant to be fully human in terms of being a person for others and of being a person whose very nature it was to give of himself throughout his life.

In all these ways, Jesus showed us the nature of God, and thus we can say with assurance that the Father himself is good, loving, and self-giving. He showed this in that he gave his only Son for us so that we might have life through him.[19]

But what of happiness? What is happiness? What is the fullness of human happiness? And is happiness related to holiness?

We know from our experience of everyday life that there is happiness and there is unhappiness, there is peace of heart and there is agitation of heart, there is the experience of loving another and being loved by another and there is loneliness. Each of these experiences of life is related to happiness and unhappiness.

What is the underlying thing that is satisfied or unsatisfied in each of these experiences of life? Is it not that our hearts know what they are created for? Is it not that our own humanity knows that it is created for happiness and it knows when it is not happy? Is it not that our hearts are restless until they achieve that which makes them happy? Therefore, can we not look at the real things in life that provide happiness and deduce therefrom what it is that gives happiness to the human heart?

When we feel safe and secure, we have some peace of heart. When we feel part of what's going on, we feel "at home" and that things are as they should be. When we

---

19    1 John 4:9 "God's love for us was revealed when God sent into the world his only Son so that we could have life through him."

feel love for another and when we feel loved, we feel all is well. Isn't it when these things are missing from our lives that we feel out of place, disturbed, and that all is not as it should be?

Other things that contribute to happiness are when we feel we have purpose in our living and that our lives have direction. When these are lacking, we feel the difference: we feel that things aren't as they should be; we feel a certain restlessness until these things are in place. Also, we feel a certain incompletion in our lives until we find these things.

When we look at all these things, we can put our finger on what it is that provides happiness for us. It is that we are made for certain things and that our hearts know when these things are not realized in us. It is only when they are realized that our hearts are at peace and happiness is the consequence.

This can be summed up in a short sentence. Happiness comes to us when we are most ourselves. Shakespeare said, "To thine own self be true."[20] We have heard it said often that we have to "find ourselves." Jesus said, "Peace be with you."

Now, to tie happiness to holiness: they have the same root. God made us for himself, and put within us that same heart-knowledge that led St. Augustine to say, "Our hearts are restless, Lord, until they rest in Thee." Since God made us to have life with him and that this life leads to fullness of life, then it is in *this* fullness of life that we find our ultimate happiness. When we look at the things that provide happiness—security, being part of what is

---

20   Hamlet

going on, loving and being loved, having purpose and direction—we come to know that each and every one of these things is exactly what we find in life with God. The very things that provide happiness in life are exactly the things that provide happiness superabundantly in life with God. Indeed, all of these things are integral to life with God. We could say that he made us in such a way as these needs of ours find their perfect answer in God. *Complete happiness is found in God, complete holiness is found in God, and God provides both to those who love him.*

But this only makes sense when we consider a little more what each is. The fullness of goodness is in God, the very nature of God is love, and self-giving is what comes out of his nature. God, out of his goodness and love, wants to give himself to us, his creation, in such a way as to fulfill all our deepest needs. God and man are made to go hand and hand in such a way that God totally completes the human person. God, in his holiness, gives himself to us in such a way as to bring about the deepest joy in our beings.

In so doing, he creates goodness, love, and self-giving in us, so that we are fully the images of him he created us to be. It is like a process of osmosis, where the nature of the one passes to the other for those who are in communion with God. And all that the fall of man produced—the movement of man out of the grace of God—is overcome as fully as possible in this life through communion with God in Christ, and totally in the life to come. Goodness, love, and self-giving are brought about in this life as much as we allow life with God here and totally in the life to come when we are fully in God's presence.

"This is what God asks of you: only this, to act justly, to love tenderly, and to walk humbly with your God."[21] To be happy is to be holy. Or, put it another way, be holy and you will be happy. God is saying to each of us, "Be good; be loving; give of yourself to others as Jesus gave of himself for all." "This is my commandment: love one another as I have loved you."[22] "You shall love Yahweh your God with all your heart, with all your soul, with all your strength. Let these words be written on your heart."[23]

All of these things prescribe God's law of happiness for us, and show us the way to holiness. We are all called to holiness; we are all called to the happiness that flows from holiness and that has its origin in God and in his desire for us to participate in his life.

---

21  Micah 6:8
22  John 15:12
23  Deuteronomy 6:5–6

# 10

## HAPPY IS GOD

For some reason or other, the image of a happy God is not one of the foremost images we have. Holy God, yes; omnipotent God, yes; angry God, yes; merciful God, yes; loving God, yes; creator God, yes; saving God, yes; happy God, not so much.

It's hard to put the "happy face" image to God; it just doesn't seem to connect. God is more serious than that, more complete, more purposeful. And yet, when we understand the nature of happiness, we discover that God is the happiest being there is; indeed, God is the very author of happiness because, like love, happiness is in God's very nature. God is love. God is happy.

The primary way we have of looking at happiness is in looking at what we identify as human happiness. To try to define divine happiness is another matter. The only visible example of divine happiness is through looking at Jesus, but his life does not really delve into what constitutes his happiness. His statement, "My peace I give you," does not really get inside what constitutes the peace he has, but if we could get "inside" his peace, we would be closer to what constitutes the happiness of God. Still, we would be looking at the human dimension of Jesus' happiness, and we would still not fully be in touch with what constitutes the happiness of God.

Does the Word of God help us, then, to delve into the nature of God's happiness so that we can come to a better understanding of it, and thus come to know that God is indeed happy, that our own happiness is something that bears a resemblance to his happiness and that our eternal happiness comes from our final "divinization" that results from coming face-to-face with him in heaven? It is, in effect, this total participation in God's life that transforms us in such a way that we "take on" his nature, take on his love, his peace, his self-giving, his happiness.

Some statements in Scripture do help us to get closer to the nature of God, help to describe him in ways we can understand and even feel.

Here are a few. Let us begin with, "You shall love Yahweh your God with all your heart, with all your soul, with all your strength. Let these words be written on your heart."[24] Here is the first commandment God has given us: love God. Love is the first thing God has told us about what is important in human life, in what we are to be and how we are to be: "with all your heart, with all your soul, with all your strength." Here God is telling us what the most

---

24   Deuteronomy 6:5–6

important thing is in our lives. Here he is telling us why, in fact, we were created: to dwell in love, to live in love, to live out of love. Happiness is connected to living in love.

Jesus would later tell us again the same thing, when he encounters Peter on the shore after the resurrection. Peter had denied Jesus three times, and instead of flailing Peter and banishing him from his presence for this most deeply hurtful action, Jesus comes to the heart of the matter. Jesus knew that Peter acted out of fear and that his action did not deny his love for Jesus. And so he comes to the point:

"After the meal Jesus said to Simon, 'Simon, son of John, do you love me more than these others do?'

"He answered, 'Yes, Lord, you know that I love you.'

"Jesus said to him, 'Feed my lambs.'

"A second time he said to him, 'Simon, son of John, do you love me?'

"He replied, 'Yes, Lord, you know I love you.'

"Jesus said to him, 'Look after my sheep.'

"Then he said to him a third time, 'Simon, son of John, do you love me?'

"Peter was upset that he asked him the third time, 'Do you love me?' and said, 'Lord, you know everything; you know I love you.'

"Jesus said, 'Feed my sheep.'"[25]

Here Jesus sets the principle criteria for his followers: "Do you love me?" We can only imagine what Peter was

---

25   John 21:15–17

feeling when Jesus met him and then asked him these questions. Even while he was asking them, Peter must have felt Jesus' forgiveness, his acceptance, and finally, at some point, understanding that what Jesus was telling him was important.

Earlier at the Last Supper, Jesus had already said, "Love one another as I have loved you."[26] The very essence of what Jesus commands, similar to what God had commanded in the first commandment, was love.

And later, St. John would repeat the primacy of love in the mind and heart of God, when he said, "My dear people, let us love one another since love comes from God and everyone who loves is begotten by God and knows God. Anyone who fails to love can never have known God, because God is love. God's love for us was revealed when God sent into the world his only Son so that we could have life through him; this is the love I mean: not our love for God, but God's love for us when he sent his Son to be the sacrifice that takes our sins away. We ourselves have known and put our faith in God's love toward ourselves. God is love, and anyone who lives in love lives in God, and God lives in him."[27]

St. Paul provides a rich look into the nature of love when he wrote to the Christians at Corinth: "And if I even let them take my body to burn it, but am without love, it will do me no good whatever. Love is always patient and kind; love is never boastful or conceited; it is never rude or selfish; it does not take offense, and is not resentful. Love takes no pleasure in other people's sins but delights in the truth; it is always ready to excuse, to trust, to hope,

---

26 John 15:12
27 1 John 4:7–10,16

and to endure whatever comes. Love does not come to an end."[28] Although Paul is speaking of human love, he is also speaking simply of the nature of love, and God is love, his nature is love, and these attributes of love apply to him as well.

The relationship between love and happiness is the key to understanding the deepest dimensions of our heart. Peace and joy and wholeness of being are interconnected attributes of the person who loves, and these are the qualities of happiness. The heart that is whole is the heart that is able to love, that is free to love. How else could it be possible for Jesus, in the midst of his agony, to have the freedom of heart and clarity of mind to say, "Father, forgive them; they do not know what they are doing."[29] This tallies with what is said of God: "You are a God of forgiveness, gracious and loving, slow to anger, abounding in goodness."[30]

Happiness is a state of the heart that is a core condition that is unmoved by circumstances. For example, we may be angered at the injustice of some event, but that transitory feeling does not supersede the actual state of heart if it is at peace, if it is suffused with joy. Long after the injustice has been rectified or the person forgiven, the state of the heart that is at peace remains so.

Another example: when one of our children is in an accident and we worry about their well being, our trust in God doesn't falter, our faith doesn't fall to pieces, nor our love for God quiver. For the soul in love with God, the circumstances of life don't alter the basic serenity of

---

28     1 Corinthians 13:3–8
29     Luke 23:34
30     Nehemiah 9:17

one's heart. It doesn't mean that we aren't concerned for our children or have anger at injustice. It means the state of our heart does not rely on these things but rather on the rock of peace and serenity of heart that comes from relationship with God. It is the very peace and serenity that is in God being passed to us through this relationship.

Jesus spoke of this tranquility of spirit when he said, "You are not to worry about your life and what you are to eat, nor about your body and how you are to clothe it. For life means more than food, and the body more than clothing. Think of the ravens. They do not sow or reap; they have no storehouses and no barns; yet God feeds them. You must not set your hearts on things to eat and things to drink; nor must you worry. It is the pagans of this world who set their hearts on these things. Your Father well knows you need them. No; set your hearts on his kingdom, and these other things will be given you as well. There is no need to be afraid, little flock, for it has pleased your Father to give you the kingdom."[31]

No worry; rather, peace of heart, confidence in the Father, trust in the goodness of God: "It has pleased your Father to give you the kingdom." Aren't all of these things a sign of the state of God's own heart?

Again, Isaiah speaks of the great banquet: "On this mountain, Yahweh Sabaoth will prepare a banquet of rich food, a banquet of fine wines, of food rich and juicy, of fine strained wines. On this mountain, he will remove the mourning veil covering all peoples, and the shroud enwrapping all nations, he will destroy Death forever. The Lord Yahweh will wipe away the tears from every cheek; he will take away his people's shame everywhere on earth,

---

31   Luke 12:22–24,29–32

*Happiness Is*

for Yahweh has said so. That day it will be said: See, this is our God in whom we hoped for salvation."[32] Is not the Eucharist itself a foretaste of that heavenly communion with God that will be total?

So, then, what exactly constitutes the nature of God's happiness that gives rise to the images provided above? It is this: at the very heart of God is peace. The peace Jesus speaks of is the very peace of God. Before any other condition of the heart, so to speak, God is peaceful of heart.

How can this be compared to the human heart? It is possible for the human heart to have an unwavering peace, no matter the circumstances that may give rise to momentary anger, elation, frustration, or other similar emotions. The peace spoken of comes from an unfaltering knowledge that God is God and is taking care of the things he has told us he would take care of when we are his.

"It has pleased your Father to give you the kingdom." This is a kingdom of light, love, forgiveness, and living each moment in the presence and care of God. It is to live in the deep knowledge that we are his children and of the deep love he has for us. This knowledge, coupled with the repeated experience of his presence in our lives, gives the human heart the ultimate peace, the rest that St. Augustine speaks of. This is the human heart, and these are the kinds of things it needs to give it this peace.

But with God, peace is the nature of his heart. Peace and love and joy are the nature of the heart of God. And this is the prevailing condition, even though God becomes angry at human injustice and evil. In heaven, this condition of

---

32   Isaiah 25:6–9

human fallen-ness does not exist, and the fullness of God's love and peace and joy are the qualities that permeate and saturate the nature of life with God. His life permeates and saturates the lives of all those who are in his presence. Peace and love and joy: these are the words that describe the happiness that is in God, that is God. We don't have words greater than these to describe the happiness of God, but it is a happiness that we, even in our human condition, come to experience now when we live in his grace, in his presence, and in his will each day.

It is clear that Jesus had this same peace of heart that is in the Father. "The Father and I are one."[33] "As the Father has loved me, so I have loved you."[34] "I have told you all this so that you may find peace in me. In the world you will have trouble, but be brave: I have conquered the world."[35] He said these words while he was still with them at the Last Supper. But when he said to them, "Peace be with you," after he had risen, he showed them his hands and his side and repeated his statement: "Peace be with you." He was speaking now out of his new state of being as the Risen One. He had entered into the new and eternal state of his being, and here is where we hear the words of the Risen Lord, fully in communion with the Father, fully one in being with the Father. The very first words he says to them are, "Peace be with you." Here he speaks of the bedrock state of his being, the very bedrock state of God's own being.

Happy is God.

---

33  John 10:30
34  John 15:9
35  John 16:33

# 11

~

# HAPPY THE ANGELS AND SAINTS

Peace and love and joy pervade heaven. This is the very state of divine happiness that is in God and in those who see him face to face, for they have become one with him in the state of their beings. Exultation, worship, praise, and thanksgiving are the things that mark what proceeds from the state of their being. They have come to the very thing God had created them for: full union with him, full communion with him, total wholeness of being. No more tears, no more fears, no more fallen-ness, no more partial-ness, no more separation, no more sin, no more evil. We can scarcely imagine it.

But let us try to imagine it. In heaven, we have God, Father and Son, the angels, and the saints. All the angels and saints are filled with the peace, love, and joy that come from God as a gift, as his desire to give his life to others, or put another way, to have others share in his life, fully share in his life.

The angels have always been in his immediate presence and shared in his life. As created beings, they have that spirit in them of praise and worship which flows from having a "heart" that is like God's, given to them by God. But they know they have been created by him to share in his life and to serve him. The spirit in them is a spirit of wonder and awe and of peace and joy and of thanksgiving and praise. They serve willingly and out of love.

What do they do? We can see from some of the instances in Scripture that they come as his messengers. Examples of this are their appearances to Mary to announce that she is to bear a Son[36] and to the shepherds to announce his arrival.[37] "And suddenly with the angel there was a great throng of the heavenly host, praising God and singing: 'Glory to God in the highest heaven, and peace to men who enjoy his favor.'"[38] Here we see them expressing joy and praise and proclaiming peace to those who enjoy God's favor. The angel warns Joseph in a dream to leave Bethlehem and flee.[39] We see them taking care of Jesus after his temptation in the wilderness[40] and again in the garden of Gethsemane to give him strength,[41] so we see that they are capable of caring and of helping. And we know of the tradition of guardian angels who are involved with us here on earth every day.

---

| 36 | Luke 1:27–38 |
| 37 | Luke 2:8–12 |
| 38 | Luke 2:13–14 |
| 39 | Matthew 2:13 |
| 40 | Matthew 4:11 |
| 41 | Luke 22:43 |

*Happiness Is*

The angels seem to have the same characteristics of how we think of the saints in heaven. They are active in heaven and on earth; they express the things we have been talking about, the very things that make up divine happiness: peace, joy, love, praise, thanksgiving, giving of self, fullness of life. When we consider the saints in heaven, we have the same image of fullness of life and happiness. Let us look at some images of the saints in heaven.

The litany of saints—that beautiful, awe-inspiring prayer of the church, sung at the Easter Vigil—says so much about the heavenly realm and our belief in their active presence. "Saints of God in glory, be with us, rejoice with us, sing praise with us, and pray with us now. Mary, mother of Jesus, Joseph, John the Baptist, Peter, Paul, Andrew, Luke, James, John, Mary of Magdala, Martha ... all women and men of the Gospel, saints of God in glory, be with us."

Here again we see the active presence of the saints in glory at work among us. Here again, we are reminded of the saints and of their continuing work in the realm of grace. They continue to be channels of God's grace for us, except now the saints are transformed by their being in God's very presence. They no longer have to surmise what that presence means to them; they no longer have to look through eyes that are only partially opened to God's reality, to his nature, that have been informed by God's own self-disclosure to us here on earth. Then, they see face to face and feel the enormity of his peace, love, and joy. They themselves are now permeated by it and transformed most fully into his likeness.

And so we see the angels and saints, though created as different beings, sharing in the one pervasive reality of heaven and that is being in God's direct presence. They share in his love for mankind; they understand fully the reason for creation, and they know who God is and what he intended for man from the beginning, and that is to share in his very life. They know the enormity of what this means for eternity, and they know the unbelievable consequence for those who place themselves outside of this life, of what they are missing in terms of eternal happiness. But the angels and saints share in God's concern and love for man and continue to be instruments of his love for man and will continue so long as mankind exists on earth.

Are there examples of this in history, examples of saints intervening for us or praying for us, or being used by God for some specific purpose for us? And do these examples tell us anything of the state of the saints being in heaven? Here are three stories that exemplify what is being said here about life in heaven.

The first is about St. Catherine of Siena. St. Catherine was born in Siena, Italy, in 1347 and died in 1380, and was named a Doctor of the Church[42] in 1970.

"She had her first vision of Christ when she was six. At fifteen, she joined the Dominicans as a layperson, continuing to live at home. Her predominant concerns were for the reform of the church, including the clergy, and the return of the Pope to Rome (he was living in France at this time when there was a schism in the church). She attracted a following of both men and women and embarked upon an apostolate that necessitated much

---

[42] A title conferred on thirty-three saints who distinguished themselves through the orthodoxy of their theological teaching. "The Doctors of the Church greatly influenced Christian thought down to the late Middle Ages."

traveling to various parts of Italy. Her life was filled with extraordinary mystical phenomena such as visions and revelations, infused knowledge, raptures, mystical espousal and marriage, and stigmata, which appeared on her body only after she died."[43]

Much has been written about St. Catherine and what she accomplished in and for the church in her short thirty-three years of life. For a person who had little or no education, she was an extraordinary person in her ability to deal with members of the church at every level. But it isn't her earthly life that is of interest here. Rather, it is about her love of God that began on earth at such depth and continued on in heaven. It was her love of God that marked her sanctity. Even more, it was her union with God that was made so manifest in what she did, what she said, and what she accomplished. She is a Doctor of the church because her sanctity is deemed to be so authentic of what God does in some of his people. In her writings, she laid bare her love of Christ and her love of the Father, and she laid bare the substance and effect of their love for her.

It is not exaggeration to say that she was filled with the love of God as much as any person has been in the life of the church. As much as anyone on earth, she knew the inner being of God because he saw fit to share his life with her to such an extent. It isn't that we need to aspire to her level of union with God, but she shows us that union with God is possible, and that union with God is the ultimate purpose of our lives. She showed us that the more she fell in love with God, the more she wanted to love him because the love she experienced was so sweet and so pervasive and

---

[43] Excerpts taken from *Saints of the Roman Calendar*. Enzo Lodi, translated and adapted by Jordan Aumann, OP. Alba House, New York, 1992, p. 101–103.

so dominant in her life. Love of God for her and her love of God showed everyone who is aware of her life that this is where God is leading all of us to, ultimately.

In heaven, she ceased having visions and ecstasies and messages. There is no need because what she saw and felt dimly, by comparison, she experiences now in fullness. The depth of love she experienced is a constant state of being for her now. And because God gifted her with concern for the church and for its priests and pastors and people, we can bet that she carries on this concern in heaven but at a deeper level than she was ever able to have on earth.

And is she happy in heaven? This is a person that lived so much in the ecstasy of love with her Lord and God that no greater image of happiness of heart, mind, and spirit can be given by someone so privileged with this foretaste of heaven. Is she happy in heaven? Even at the level of her earthly experience of God, this is still but a blurred image of the fullness of love to be experienced in heaven and with it the knowledge of reality that flows from that life with God.

The second saint that gives us an image of heaven is St. Blaise. "According to the Latin Martyrology, the feast of St. Blaise is celebrated on the day of his death (beheaded Feb. 3, 316). Biographical details are very scarce. It is said that a mother came to the bishop (of Sebaste in Armenia), asking him to cure her son, who was choking on a fish bone stuck in his throat, and the bishop saved the child with a prayer and the sign of the cross.

For that reason St. Blaise is venerated as patron of those suffering from diseases of the throat. In many churches of the Latin rite, two blessed candles are tied together in the form of St. Andrew's cross and applied to the throat as the priest pronounces a special invocation to St. Blaise to protect the individual against diseases of the throat. In the Opening Prayer of the Mass, we ask God, through the intercession of St. Blaise, to give us the joy of his peace in this life and eternal happiness in heaven. In the Italian Missal, the request is for 'peace and health,' thus recognizing the widespread confidence in St. Blaise as a healer. If St. Blaise is invoked as a powerful intercessor for the health of the body, it is because he was a martyr for the church."[44]

Here we see the centuries-old tradition of the church in its belief in the active participation on earth of the saints in heaven. The Mystical Body of Christ participates with the Lord in his saving work on earth, and this mission does not cease when one enters heaven. Each of the saints will have their continuing role to pray for people on earth. Here we see that St. Blaise has been interceding for centuries for the benefit of people's health.

But we see also, in the opening prayer of the Mass on his feast, that St. Blaise is asked to intercede for us in asking God to give us the joy of God's peace in this life and eternal happiness in heaven. The history and tradition of the church asks all the saints to intercede for us because they are powerful intercessors, and they are so because they are in the immediate presence of God and abound in the life that God gives.

The last saint to look at is St. Gertrude. St. Gertrude lived from 1256 to 1302. "At age 5 she entered the Benedictine Monastery, where she was educated and later professed as a nun. At age 26 she received the first of the

---

44   Ibid., p.39–41.

revelations for which she is famous. She was extremely devoted to the mystery of the Incarnation, expressed in the Sacred Heart of Jesus and the holy Eucharist (she promoted frequent Communion). She authored several spiritual works although they were not discovered until 1536, after which her influence spread throughout Europe.

"The opening prayer of her feast day Mass touches on the essential themes in the spirituality of this great German mystic. 'Father, you filled the heart of St. Gertrude with the presence of your love. Bring light into our darkness and let us experience the joy of your presence and the power of your grace.' In her treatise, *Herald of Divine Love*, she states that Christ said to her: 'I want your writings to be indisputable evidence of my goodness.' The relevance of this 'herald of divine love,' as Christ named her, is her intimate union with Christ and her devotion to the Sacred Heart of Jesus."[45]

Here is another saint that experienced in her own being the very love of Christ, and she witnessed to that experience and the knowledge of love that comes from it in her writings. So clear and powerful were these writings that they became acclaimed as true witnesses to the divine love of Christ, a love that mirrors the love of the Father, and spurred on a devotion to the Sacred Heart, the Sacred Love, of Jesus. And through her witness, Christ obtained the indisputable evidence of his goodness.

Today, seven centuries later, people still feast on the love of God found in her words. One can imagine that she herself prays that Christ will let countless numbers of ordinary men and women on earth experience the

---

45    Ibid., p.356–7.

depth and treasure of his love. Indeed, this would be the common prayer of the heavenly host, angels and saints, because of their moment-by-moment living in that love and peace and joy.

# 12

~

# BE HAPPY

With all these thoughts in mind, we can again visit the Beatitudes to see what treasure they contain as statements of what constitutes, at the practical, everyday level, happiness for the human soul. Happiness *is* something, *contains* something, and *expresses* something that is understandable and desirable. If we want to be truly happy, with a happiness that is not subject to the circumstances of daily life and events, there is no greater place to look than the Beatitudes. They just need a few keys to open the door to their treasure.

The first key is to look at these statements as coming from God, as representing God's goal for us: happiness—true, immovable happiness, happiness not subject to changing conditions or circumstance, a bedrock type of happiness that is the true condition of our hearts and not something that is an act.

The second key to understanding these statements is to know that Jesus knew what he was talking about. He was in communion with his Father, and he knew what this happiness is that he spoke of. He knew the joy and peace and love that are in the Father; he had them in himself, and he knew the Father's will for all mankind—that we are to share in the Father's life through Jesus. When we are in communion with Jesus, he brings us into communion with the Father, and the fruit of this is the happiness promised in these statements—how we are to be happy in spirit and truth, in this life and the next.

Simple belief in God does not bring this about. Simple rule-following for living doesn't bring this about. Communion with God brings this about. It is this communion with God that is the hallmark of the kingdom of God. All the words of the Beatitudes have to be seen in this light: they are totally about the kingdom of God. With this in mind, let us look at each beatitude and see how it reflects the mind and heart of God in his desire for us.

*How happy are the poor in spirit; theirs is the kingdom of God.* The kingdom of God belongs to the poor in spirit. What does poor in spirit mean? And how is it linked to the kingdom of God? Let's begin with the latter. The kingdom of God exists where God is central, where he is at the heart of communion between all who are in the kingdom. When this is so, God's own mind and spirit pervades and motivates the whole kingdom. God is first in the hearts and minds of all; God's own happiness, his peace and love and joy, permeate the hearts, minds, and spirits of all; God's purpose is known and understood; God's will is known and understood, rejoiced in, and sought; the spirit of praise and thanksgiving abounds; fullness of life is experienced and pressed toward.

The poor in spirit are those who are attached to God alone and nothing else. Their happiness derives from God's own life and from his very presence within their souls at work in them, producing, little by little, more of the spirit and mind of the kingdom in them, until they are remade more in the image of God's own being.

When we are attached to other things, no matter what it may be—money, possessions, the search for a better life through material means or work or power—these in themselves can never bring us the happiness that comes from communion with God. At their worst, they produce a state of being that can keep us from ever looking to God for happiness. They divert our gaze away from God. This is the first beatitude because it deals with the most seductive of illusions in life, illusions that keep us from communion with God. None of these things has to be such a diversion; they can be part of what God had given us to exercise stewardship over, but they become the means for being separated from God when we attach ourselves to them in spirit, where they displace God as first in our lives.

Why does the kingdom of heaven belong to those who are in communion with God? It is because it is through this communion that the kingdom is brought about. It is because the natural consequence of being in communion with God is the creation, by God, of the ingredients of the kingdom in our own souls, the very life that is in God.

*Happy the meek, they shall have the earth for their heritage.* Happy the meek; the earth for their heritage: what does each part mean? What is the connection?

The meek person is the humble person who knows who he is before God. He knows he is God's beloved child, and he knows who others are in relation to God. He has a disposition that treats another person as God's beloved. This is God's own point of view toward each of us. We are his people, his beloved: "Does a woman forget the baby at her breast, or fail to cherish the son within her womb? Yet, even if these forget, I will never forget you. See, I have branded you on the palm of my hand."[46] Indeed, the humble gentleness of the mother with her child is the great image here of the love of God for us, his children. For the meek and humble of heart, this becomes their spirit toward others, too. When the love of God permeates our spirit, it produces this meekness, this humility and gentleness, toward all people who are now seen as the "apple of God's eye."

The earth spoken of is the kingdom of heaven equivalent to the land promised to the Israelites: "I have resolved to bring you up out of Egypt where you are oppressed, into a land of milk and honey."[47] Like the first beatitude, the kingdom is the natural consequence for those who act justly, love tenderly, and walk humbly with their God.[48] This is to live daily in the immediate presence of God, aware of his presence and his love, and rejoicing in his will for our lives. This is meekness at its best, humility in its reality, and love in essence. The kingdom of God in all its

---

46    Isaiah 49:15–16
47    Exodus 3:17
48    Micah 6:8

fullness will be its heritage; participation in the kingdom of God is its present experience.

Jesus himself was the best example for us, "Come to me, all you who labor and are overburdened, and I will give you rest. Shoulder my yoke and learn from me, for I am meek and humble of heart, and you will find rest for your souls. Yes, my yoke is easy and my burden light."[49]

*Happy those who mourn, they shall be comforted.* There is a mourning for which there is no comfort, a mourning that eats away at the human soul: a mourning that robs life of its happiness. It is mourning that is done within the human condition alone, where God is not involved. But where God is involved, life and death have different meaning; life abounds with hope and love; faith has meaning that actually affects life and sees it through the tough patches of life; God is in the present and future, giving both meaning beyond current sadness and grief.

God gives meaning to death that, beyond mourning, brings the comfort of joy and peace. In our love for those near to us, we must be sad, we must feel our grief, and we must be comforted by those around us who love us. But all the while, we know, even in the deepest part of our grief, that God's loving and healing presence is with us. God gives us comfort no other can; he brings us through these times with a total sense of his reality and his purpose, and these give us comfort.[50]

*Happy those who hunger and thirst for what is right, they shall be satisfied.* Within the spirit of God is the hunger and thirst

---

[49] Matthew 11:28–30
[50] Psalm 23:4 "Though I pass through a gloomy valley, I fear no harm; beside me your rod and your staff are there, to hearten me."

for what is right. It is part of his love for us that when love is betrayed or offended against, the love of God seeks what is right to be done. In that frame of reference, we see God's own ability to forgive us what we do regularly against love, against those we love, and against those we don't know. We see the daily acts against love throughout the world and wonder what can ever make these things right. For those who are in the love of God, his own desire for righteousness in us rubs off on us and produces that holy desire that righteousness in people prevail, that goodness and love prevail, that goodwill toward all prevail. We seek it in our families, in our neighborhoods, in our communities, in our cities and nations, and in our world.

Those who have this hunger and thirst will be satisfied, says the Lord. And not just when they pass into heaven, but here in this world; just like those who mourn will be comforted by God in this world, so too will those who hunger and thirst for what is right be satisfied in this life by God. He will do this by giving eyes to see when righteousness has been brought about, and thankfulness for being able to see it. Sometimes, they themselves will be instruments for bringing about righteousness and will be able to rejoice at what God had brought about through the desire he himself has given them.

*Happy the merciful, they shall have mercy shown them.* Where would we be if not for the mercy of God? It is God, in his love for us, who brought about the means of our salvation, the means of our being able to enter into communion with him. Every time God forgives each of us for what we do, he shows his mercy. Mercy is such a component of the nature of God's love as to be inseparable from it. Mercy and compassion are the marks of God's love. When we are in communion with God, he brings about this quality of love in us; we become the visible signs of his mercy to those around us because of the state of heart he has brought about in us.

Mercy is so connected to our ability to forgive that what Jesus says in the Lord's Prayer applies to mercy. "Forgive us our trespasses as we forgive those who trespass against us."

Jesus' story of the unforgiving debtor makes this point.

"And so the kingdom of heaven may be compared to a king who decided to settle accounts with his servants. When the reckoning began, they brought him a man who owed ten thousand talents, but he had no means of paying, so his master gave orders that he should be sold, together with his wife and children and all his possessions, to meet the debt. At this, the servant threw himself down at his master's feet. 'Give me time,' he said, 'and I will pay the whole sum.' And the servant's master felt so sorry for him that he let him go and cancelled the debt."

But the servant turned around and demanded payment to him by those who owed him, and he wouldn't forgive their debt and had them put in prison until they paid him. When the master heard what had happened, he sent for him.

"'You wicked servant,' he said, 'I cancelled all that debt of yours when you appealed to me. Were you not bound, then, to have pity on your fellow servant just as I had pity on you?' And in his anger, the master handed him over to the torturers till he should pay all his debt. And that is how my heavenly Father will deal with you unless you each forgive your brother from your heart."[51]

*Happy the pure in heart, they shall see God.* Those already in heaven are pure in heart because they see God, and the sight of God is both transformative and preoccupying. They cannot *not* see God. He is there in full view, face to face. They see him in all his beauty; they experience the purity of his love, they experience his peace; they know what being in his presence is like; they are able to think properly because of the love he enables them to have, unencumbered by the things from which they have been freed in this life that lead us astray.

The pure in heart in this life are able to see God in the ways human beings are capable of seeing God. It is not face to face, but it affects their lives nonetheless. The gift of sight given by God is a gift to be able to see with the "eyes of the heart," with the related understanding given to the mind, and with a spirit resembling that of heaven because it contains the elements of peace, love, and joy.

The pure in heart are able to put God first in their affection, in their purpose, and in their daily lives. It is a two-edged sword: the pure in heart are able to see God, and those able to see God are given purer hearts. This most beautiful beatitude speaks to the clarity of what true communion with God brings, and in this life we are enabled to have a foretaste of the heavenly kingdom. The communion of saints has its foundation in this beatitude, and the purity of the kingdom on earth has its most effective cause in this beatitude.

---

51    Matthew 18:23–35

*Happy the peacemakers, they shall be called sons of God.* To be a peacemaker in this sense doesn't first and foremost mean being a bridge between opposing factions of people. What it means is to be a spreader of the peace of God in the hearts of men and women. Just as this peace is the consequence of the peace of Christ and comes through union and communion with him, so too does the spread of this peace come as a consequence of others being brought into union with Christ. This beatitude is the foundation and fruit of evangelization.

Those who are peacemakers are sons and daughters of God because they replicate the very actions of Jesus. The Gospel of Christ is the very source of peace of heart and spirit. His own life was the very image of this peace of heart, and his actions showed his followers how they, too, were to be "fishers of men."[52] This is, in effect, to spread the kingdom of God, a kingdom marked by communion with God and its resultant peace, love, and joy. This is the true kingdom Jesus came to give, and not just when he was on earth, but for the rest of time. The men and women who are in union with Christ are the true peacemakers in the world because of their communion with God.

*Happy those who are persecuted in the cause of right, theirs is the kingdom of heaven. Happy are you when people abuse you and persecute you and speak all kinds of calumny against you on my account. Rejoice and be glad, for your reward will be great in heaven; this is how they persecuted the prophets before you.* No greater example exists of the contrast between the logic of God and the logic of man than is seen in this beatitude. Who could think that one could rejoice and be glad when one is abused or persecuted? And yet this is what Jesus tells

---

52  Mark 1:17

us about those who are so treated because of their life with him. We see how he was treated and how his apostles were treated. We see how his disciples throughout the centuries have been treated. We see how his followers are treated in this day and age.

Why is this so? Why is it so inevitable?

It is because we have our life in God through Christ, and those who reject God and/or Christ will reject us. But, in this sense, the treatment, good or ill, received by Christians is secondary to their real life of communion with God. This is their real home, their real life, and their real motivation. The love of God compels them through their union with him. They know his reality; they know the reality of who God is; they know his purpose; they know his goodness and his power to forgive; they know his desire for all people to be in union with him made possible through Christ.

"Rejoice and be glad, for your reward will be great in heaven." In this life, when we are in communion with God, we are to rejoice and be glad. This is to be the state of our hearts no matter what is happening in our lives because we are living in God and we are living in Christ and through Christ. Rejoice and be glad because we are one with God in our daily lives. "Yet do not rejoice that the Spirits submit to you; rejoice rather that your names are written in heaven."[53] So it is not how we are received or treated by others but how God himself receives us and what he wills for us that is the key matter. We are to love all, no matter the treatment accorded us. We are to be true to ourselves, which means to be true to our real union with

---

53    Luke 10:20

*Happiness Is*

God and what it produces in our souls, in our hearts, and in our minds and spirits.

Happiness is …

Ultimately, happiness is what we are made for. True happiness is in God and comes from God. It comes from God through communion with Him through Jesus Christ. "I am the Way, the Truth and the Life. No one can come to the Father except through me. If you know me, you know my Father too."[54] He is the source of true, everlasting happiness of the deepest order. This happiness is comprised of peace, love, and joy, and it is a happiness that is capable of enduring the most horrendous hardships in life. It is beyond the circumstances of daily life. It provides fullness of life here on earth,[55] and it continues into the next life in complete fullness.

"Father, may they be one in us, as you are in me and I am in you, so that the world may believe it was you who sent me. I have given them the glory that you have given me, that they may be one as we are one."[56]

Here is the source of happiness on earth and the first image of heaven.

---

54   John 14:6–7
55   John 10:10 "I have come so that they may have life and have it to the full. I am the good shepherd. The good shepherd is one who lays down his life for his sheep. I know my own, and my own know me, just as the Father knows me and I know the Father."
56   John 17:21–22

CPSIA information can be obtained at www.ICGtesting.com
Printed in the USA
LVOW050727270213

321809LV00001B/11/P